What is good sense? It may not be as common as you think! Arthur Dogson Todd has an uncommon form of good sense to share that is often humorous and inadvertently wise.

Coming from a rescuer's home on the Cumberland Plateau, Arthur describes himself as a "pure pup" when he arrives at Misty Meadows Farm. With his naïve nature intact, he like many young idealists runs into unfairness, misunderstanding, and even combat.

Based on actual events, a wide variety of situations, and his clever take on life, Arthur's stories provide quotable quotes, fun plays-on-words, and lively images of all sorts of battles even some within himself. Being sensitive as well as having a sensible approach to problems, he comes up with surprising observations of other residents, especially the humans whom he calls sapiens as a testament to their wisdom.

His journey toward maturity follows many paths, including bringing his case against the rooster to Judge Robin's court. In other adventures, he confronts deceptive business practices with the authority of a self-appointed Canine Representative, and also attempts to assist Mother Nature in the survival of one species.

Arthur has a lasting place as a charming, energetic, and lovable canine who strives to make his world fair and just with dignity and happiness for all.

A Canine's Memoir

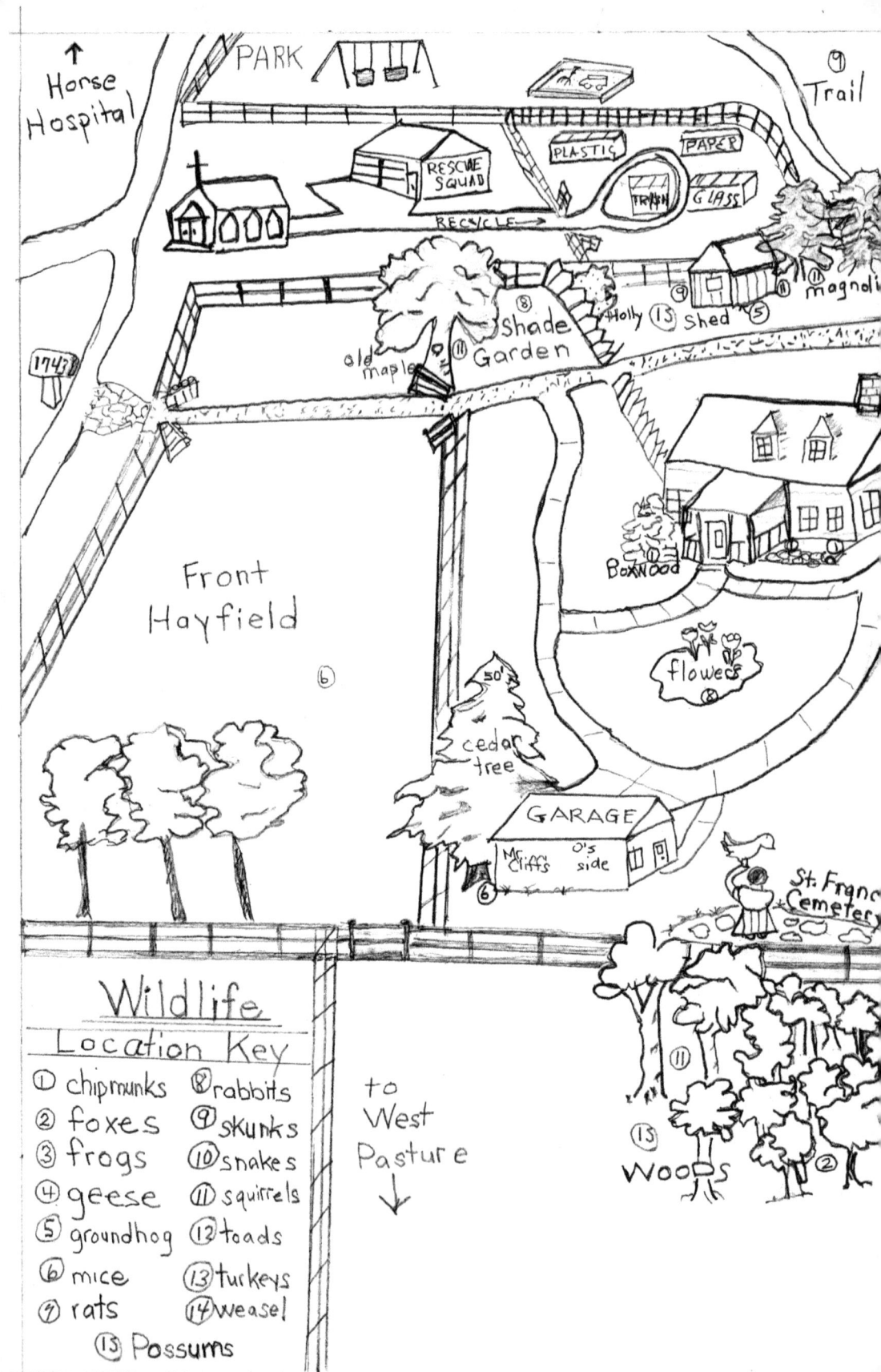

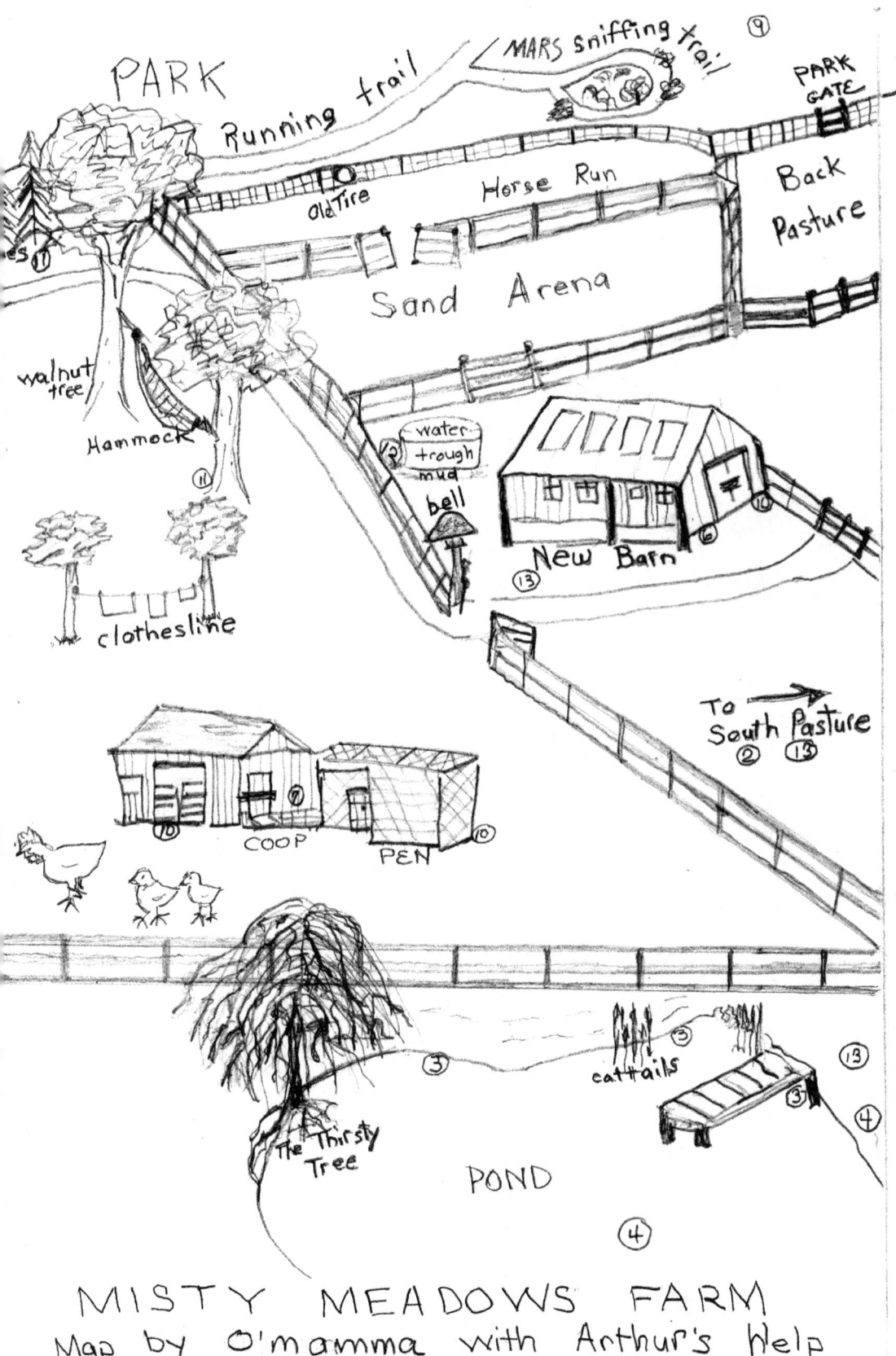

PARK

Running trail

MARS sniffing trail ⑨

PARK GATE

Old Tire

Horse Run

Back Pasture

Sand Arena

walnut tree

Hammock

② water-trough mud bell

New Barn ⑥ ⑩

⑬

clothesline

⑦ ⑩

⑯ COOP PEN

To South Pasture
② ⑬

The Thirsty Tree

③

cattails ③

③ ⑬

④

POND

④

MISTY MEADOWS FARM
Map by O'mamma with Arthur's Help

Also by Louise DeVito

Two Spirits Here

A
Canine's
Memoir

"If It Makes Sense...
It Must Be True."

By

Arthur Dogson Todd

Assisted by

Louise DeVito

A Dogson Edition

Ideas into Books: Westview®

Kingston Springs, Tennessee

Ideas into Books: Westview®
P.O. Box 605
Kingston Springs, TN 37082
www.ideasintobooks.net

ISBN 978-1-62880-272-6

This book is dedicated

to

Clifton Leon Todd

In memory of

Nancy, Antoinette, Louise and Nicholas DeVito

CONTENTS

INTRODUCTION

While on the phone with O'mamma, I heard the first words she said to Arthur, "Twenty-five more miles until we arrive at your forever home, my sleepy little guy." At Misty Meadows Farm, Sparkle and I waited by the front gate.

Down the mountain from the Cumberland Plateau had been a long journey in the rescuer's old blue van for Arthur and eleven other pups along for the ride to Nashville. As she looked through the side window, O'mamma saw tiny dogs sprawled everywhere from dashboard to floor. The kind-hearted rescuer greeted her and placed Arthur in her arms. She gave him a farewell kiss before O' put him into his new blue carrier.

Arthur was on his way to a world bigger than anything he had ever seen, twenty-two acres of fields, woods, a pond and two barns. He would have to learn about it all from the get-go. New creatures, sights, and smells, as well as foreign sounding neighs, howls, croaks, and cackles were about to flood his senses.

Within a few days, I could see that our new little Dachshund and Jack Russell mix came with his instincts, values, and dreams already in place. In a month's time, he was working hard searching for intruders, barking, and patrolling the perimeter.

It wasn't long before he made me proud. We were sitting in the truck waiting for O'mamma to come out of the grocery when he "protected" me from a man reaching through the half-open window to pet him. Without a sound, Arthur drew his lip back. I saw his teeth glisten, and the guy did too!

O'mamma and I, his sapiens, recognized how sharp he was. So, we let him follow us around and talked to him about everything he saw. Arthur caught on fast to "what was what" on the farm.

If something unusual crossed his path, he perked his ears and stared at it without blinking. The first time he saw the rooster rush toward him flapping his wings, I could see the wheels in his mind turning. I laughed. I was sure he and that bird would face off one day.

Because of our admiration for his special qualities, we, The People in Charge, lost perspective and took his opinions too much to heart. I admit that we were likely too proud to be receptive to his inquiring nature because we were Sapiens, and as such, we were always right!

We began to call his observations "complaints." "Arthur's complaining again!" we said unaware that our own complaints rode the exhale of our impatient sighs dozens of times. Now, I realize he felt the stress of unfairness and inequalities that we didn't recognize.

Did he disturb our convenient and comfortable view of perfection at Misty Meadows? Yes, he did. But although his fresh take included negativity, he was usually right.

So much more than a critic, I am pleased to call Arthur a loyal canine, honest and energetic, protecting us with his wisdom and dedication. That doesn't mean he's all work and no play. He steps lightly, rolls in whatever he wants, and eats lots of extras, even smiles at times.

Early on, I remember him running through the flock of chickens for the thrill of seeing them fly up and squawk. Our eyes met, and we both laughed. I liked his style. Still do!

Free in body, mind, and spirit, Arthur has been living an unleashed life. The time has come to set aside our early judgments while he was still technically a baby. Let's forgive ourselves for our own complaints as well and enjoy his stories with the enthusiasm that an open mind and heart allow.

Mr. Cliff Todd
Misty Meadows Farm
Battle Station, Tennessee

PROLOGUE

"*L isten carefully just in case it's about you.*" I always tell myself that when they talk fast and frown.

My sapiens, Mr. Cliff and O'mamma, huddled in the living room "discussing" something important. As soon as the phrase "canine complaints" hit my ears, I knew I should go on high alert. That was the original title she came up with for this book.

When she first mentioned it, I was more than unhappy. I told them, "*Get serious, sapiens! If you tell the whole world I'm a complainer, they won't want to get to know me.*

"*Say I'm an observer and a free-thinker. Say I'm adventuresome and fun. Tell everyone I'm about facts and truth. Okay, in case you still need convincing, I'll explain one more time...*"

What I have shared in my stories is what I have discovered along the way. The facts I found were not just beautiful, sweet, and kind. Some showed what was unfair or just plain wrong and even what smelled awfully suspicious. Telling the facts was reporting, not complaining.

Fortunately, my sapiens didn't monitor and judge every move I made. I had only three rules to follow—come when called by name, be polite, and don't pee in the house. For everything else, they allowed me to follow my instincts without interference.

I became my own boss mulling over the details of tough situations and deciding what to do next. To be successful, I had to have strict guidelines. I told myself, *"Nothing should escape my scrutiny, and nothing should be ignored or forgotten."* Mr. Cliff noticed my dedication to perfection. One day, he pointed at me with the tip of his cane and declared, "That is one hard workin' dawg."

How does a canine gather precise information and draw conclusions? How can someone on four legs without a thumb find out anything? Easy! He's highly motivated by a protective nature that makes him curious, suspicious, and intense. He doggedly follows his natural instincts for danger. Sharp senses of smell and hearing make it simple to follow leads.

I've always had more free time than they did to dwell on the details of what went on minute by minute at Misty Meadows Farm. My sapiens needed theirs to work to get money for food and all the rest they bought. I spent mine protecting what they brought home. When one of us would say work takes up a lot of time, it was a fact about our efforts that gave us a sense of responsibility as well as pride.

With practice, I've become an expert farm manager. I learned to pay attention to more of this and less of that. Odors in the grass are stronger in the morning, so I focus on sniffing early in the a.m. That way, I prepare myself in case the one who was prowling last night comes back again, especially if he smelled like the dangerous kind. Squirrels are fun to chase, but they aren't dangerous. I don't spend as much time on them now.

I put the facts I find together in the most sensible way possible. Then, I offer my opinions hoping they will benefit everyone. If what I notice needs to change, that view might look negative because it really is. Occasionally, I hear what my sapiens think and change my mind. Not often, though.

In the evenings while they have their feet up looking at the news on TV, my joy at that hour is barking and chasing away "wildlife." Not one of that group dares to step foot on our farm while I'm on duty.

The kind of information required for the job I do is not on TV. I have never heard a news report that the skunks irritated by a late spring are ready to show the whole town how they feel. Has anyone ever heard a reporter say, "One dangerously hungry possum was last seen in central Battle Station trying to break into chicken pens?"

From my humble beginning, I brought dreams and ambitions with me to Misty Meadows Farm. Then I ran with all my strength toward the challenge of figuring out animal and human ways. I felt hopeful and free.

As time went on, I found that reality didn't always turn out to be what I expected. Deep disappointment filled me with pain. There was a huge gap between what I thought would be sensible and fair and what was actually happening. I solved problems I never could have imagined, especially those from the dark side of myself.

As I look back, I admit that my observations when young and new at the job were affected by personal feelings. Yes, some might be considered "overly emotional, reactive, and exaggerated," Mr. Cliff's very words about me back then. Am I forgiving of that? Yes, but only if he agrees that any professional can get too close to his work at times.

So, kind sapiens, as you read through this book, please keep in mind that I accept some of my early attempts at conclusions based on facts as unduly negative. Please don't let that stop you. Stay with me on my journey while I mature into the free-thinking observer that Mr. Cliff and O'mamma love and admire.

Respectfully,
Arthur Dogson Todd
Canine Representative (self-appointed)

CHICKEN TROUBLE

During the slowdown after lunch, I was lying on the upholstered chair near the sunroom with my head lowered onto my paws, tilted slightly toward the rug. *"Lives could be at stake. Probably not today,"* I thought, so I allowed myself to sink into oblivious relaxation.

When I'm the only canine on duty, I position myself precisely in order to make a 180-degree scan as efficiently as possible. At the moment that scents and sounds alert me to an emergency, I'm ready to spring into action.

Battle Station was enjoying a gorgeous August 22nd, most likely the best one on record. Fluffy, friendly looking clouds drifted across the afternoon sky. A slight breeze and warm temperatures made living feel easy that summer day.

Well, that was for everyone except O'mamma who thrashed about in an altered state of reality. Her head down, number crunching, paper-shuffling, tense behavior was that of someone who had submitted to the dominance of the IRS.

The impending due date for filing had created a sapiens I didn't even recognize. My Pillar of Patience was mumbling unintelligible words as a lovely breeze played with her piles of paper. Records of income drifted into expenses, and the 1099's floated to the floor.

For four months she had been comfortable with procrastination, but at three o'clock this morning O'mamma awoke in a full body sweat. In the blink of an eye, the reality of the deadline broke through her barrier of denial. Peace was washed away by turmoil. Fear stole her ability to keep the notice from the Internal Revenue Service out of mind.

Breathing deeply, imagining a peaceful place, and chanting self-reassuring mantras, all of her special strategies for fighting anxiety, withered at the sound of the keywords of the IRS—Penalties, Interest, and Jail.

Suddenly, there arose squawking and crowing and other disturbing noises known to signal that our chickens were in danger. Frantic voices of sapiens cried out, "Quick! In the park! Your chickens are over here!"

"What is wrong now? Can't those birds give it a rest?" I asked. *"All day they swarm like bees in the yard around the barn and under the magnolia row."*

O'mamma and I had to switch to animal rescue mode, like it or not. The IRS would have to wait, so she liked it. I did not. *"Did those birds choose nap time on purpose?"* I was suspicious.

"Calm yourself! Have more compassion." My conscience was scolding me as I ran. *"Chickens are hard working little critters."*

Within a few steps, an uncensored yet sensible idea jumped from my overly stressed brain. *"If I always listen to my conscience, I won't be who I am."* So, I stayed annoyed and judged them harshly.

Our standard operating procedure was to react as if there was a life-threatening emergency each and every time since we couldn't tell if it was until we got there to see for ourselves. A hen might be caught in the fence. A predator might have crossed the property line looking for chicken dinner.

O'mamma grabbed the red canvas bag that holds the CRESEK (Chicken Rescue Squad Equipment Kit), and we ran at our quickest pace toward the gate at the park boundary.

Even though I had arrived at the point of impatience, I dutifully followed her toward the rescue operation. The angry energy of disgruntled feelings fueled my determination to bring those flockers home.

When I saw the horses standing quietly gazing at the horizon as we crossed the back pasture, the irritation I felt got worse. My conscience knew, so it began mocking me with the words I chant to build my self-esteem through self-praise, *"I-like-to-be-constantly-kind."*

"Why won't you leave me alone?

"If those grazing gazers had a harder job, there wouldn't be time to pose as yard art, and I wouldn't have to listen to you!"

I threw those exact words back over my shoulder as I ran. I considered my reply sharp and strong enough, but I really wanted to say, *"Stop acting like a mocking bully."* That would have been a brilliant comeback given the amount of stress blocking the operation of half of my brain. But it would have been too risky.

Then, the magnitude of the absurdity struck me. What I had in front of me was the most sizeable conundrum I'd ever faced. Thousand-pound horses scanned the hills for predators worrying about self-preservation while four-pound chickens gleefully ran into foreign territory protected only by feathers and totally unconcerned about their safety.

"The chickens could use a little of that composure the horses have," I thought while we practically flew toward them. *"Why do they stay scattered and hysterical and never learn from their misadventures?"*

Once more, I asked, *"Is there really a Mother Nature? If she does exist, why does she make us suffer over things that don't make sense?"*

We unlocked and re-locked the gate and ran down the path in the park.

Unbelievable! Nearly the entire flock was running out of control across the park lawn pecking at bugs. *"You have plenty of bugs in your own yard,"* another harsh yet accurate judgment. I knew my conscience was listening, but it gave me great pleasure to say it, anyway.

An old tire with a hole in the middle big enough to run through was lodged in the rusted wire fence. They had found their way through the place I used to enter the park for investigation.

I was under the extreme stress of two things at once, exerting myself during my usual napping hour and having to be cautious of what I said in the fight with my conscience. Then I thought I saw the tire levitate. It was rising up out of the fence and rushing toward me like a huge spinning donut.

"Am I going crazy, or do I need a treat?" The answer was obviously *"a treat."*

With arms outstretched, O'mamma had the opened blanket held up high to make it look like a wall. Beginning on the grassy field and crossing the gravel path, she moved slowly toward them. They scattered along our fence row among trees and weeds running and screeching like we were the danger.

"Pay attention, guys and girls! We are not the enemy. We are the rescuers."

I wanted them to stop and think like I do, but I realized chickens just aren't dogs. If I don't get used to that as a fact, I'll never develop patience with their personalities. O'mamma accepts them for who they are—birds in a flock on the ground who need good fences. She says it's not the "who they are part" but the "accepts" part that gives her patience.

After most of them had found the hole in the fence and come through to our side, she folded the blanket and took up the stick with the string attached. The end of the episode came down to a final contest between her and a rooster we called Big because he was the biggest one. He tried to elude her admirably making some smart moves for a chicken.

Having practiced with that string and stick for years, O'mamma could put the string on the exact spot she wanted to anytime she wanted to. She did just that, striking the tree very close to his tail feathers. He lost his composure and got hysterical just like a sissy hen.

That's when I knew she had him. Increasing the pressure, she whacked the string on the ground grazing his wing. He fled through the fence. It was over.

We walked back from the park through the gate unlocking and re-locking it. The rush of adrenalin was waning and our mood became lighter.

Passing the horses, I paused to send them reassuring vibes. The cats in the barn saw me go by and did the respectful thing. They got out of my way.

We crossed the backyard and came into the house returning to our former positions. As I relaxed in my chair with head hanging down at the proper angle, it felt like we had never left.

WE ALL WORK

G uarding the perimeter of Misty Meadows Farm is the most important thing I do. My job is to be on alert for even a hint of an intruder and then to give notice with the Fair-Warning Bark (FWB). If that fails to stop him, I change to the next level of vocal strength, the Intruder-Alert Bark (IAB). Mr. Cliff and O'mamma can tell which one is more serious by the deeper tone of the IAB.

My assistant, Pristine, is on call to run with me chasing away the unwelcome boundary-crossers. Not much passes under the fence or goes through the gates without my knowledge. If I make a mistake and bark at the wrong person like a friend or relative, I follow up quickly with a Friendly-Greeting Bark (FGB), also known as the Forget-About-It Bark, and hope to be forgiven.

Capturing an animal and carrying him in my mouth is no longer required as part of the job. One night, I caught my first, and last, young possum. The minute I tasted his fur and felt him wiggle, I gagged. He fell out of my open mouth and ran.

O'mamma was in the barn with me, so she understood by the way I reacted that I found Direct Mouth Capture (DMC) far too repulsive. Killing is not part of my job either. Canine cuisine and treats are all I eat.

The elements of a work situation influence my mood. Often, the fluctuations from sweet to sour and gentle to fierce swung too fast and far. I needed something to help me be more even-tempered.

I had tried making a list of Rules for Action to follow as a solid step-by-step approach in an emergency, but that didn't work at all. By the time I'd read it, the problem had gotten worse, and my confidence had gone south.

O'mamma suggested this mantra to encourage a calm, common-sense approach.

My nature is the same
As the level of the threat.
What I see and what I hear
Determines what you get.

While O'mamma's working, each morning we see her in a sweet and gentle mood. She says we live "in community" and that everyone's job helps everyone else.

Our work assignments at different areas of the farm are matched up with our talents. The chickens take care of, a nice way of saying "eat," the bugs in the grass, the bushes, and the garden. When there is nothing to frighten them, their mood is happy. The whole flock sings while they work close to each other. O'Mamma calls them the pest patrol, but I call them *snackers*.

The cats are in charge of getting rid of intruders in the new barn. Theirs is only indoor work. To me, it looks like most of their time is spent waiting. They lie around looking relaxed, just gentle little kitties yawning or sleeping like babies in some strange positions even upside down.

"Just picture this... me, a canine, guarding on my back with three feet in the air and one paw tucked under my chin! Ha! Ha! Ha!"

One time O'mamma said, "You are just a furry-purry love" to Sammi. That was hard to hear because I don't trust that view of any of the cats. They are fooling her. When she's not around, they give me what Mr. Cliff calls "the squinchy-eye."

Not wanting to trigger the other side of their personalities, I may glance, but I don't stare. Who they really are must come into play on the night shift. I'll tell you something that goes unnoticed. *"There is nothing smaller than them alive at the barn."*

And then there are those big, lovable vegan guys. O'Mamma and Mr. Cliff agree that the horses "work" at cutting grass.

"Uh-h, please look more carefully. Obviously, they are eating. Everybody's 'job' is eating except for mine and Pristine's."

Once in a while, I do get a food cleanup job like the other morning when McDonald's fries were scattered outside near the kitchen door. Another day, there might be an inside spill. I volunteer as soon as I notice.

"Do they call my cleanup efforts 'work'? No."

O'mamma to Mr. Cliff, "Arthur was so lucky. He got to eat the French fries you spilled!" That was so far from fair I had to speak out...

"I saved you from bending down with a full tum-tum. So, if it's easier for me 'cuz I'm closer to the ground, you think you can call me lucky when I'm working?

"Let's get real, sapiens. 'Lucky' is for the one who gets to have the food in the first place!

"Next time, make my day! Spill it in my bowl! That's luck!

"And I won't even care if you say, 'Isn't Arthur the pluckiest-luckiest darn dawg!'"

WHAT'S IN A NAME

Part 1: The Abbey Downtown

I am lucky but that was never my name. When I arrived at Misty Meadows Farm from the Cumberland Plateau, O'mamma said she called me R.T. for "Rough and Tumble." That lasted a few years through my little cute guy days. Then it was "R'Thur." I can still feel the rhythmic start-stop beat of my name making me sound like a rapper.

Fortunately, her childhood love of opera returned, and she began saying my name, "Ar-tu-ro" rolling the r's on the tip of the tongue. Her tongue must have gotten tired of working so hard because Arturo lasted only a few weeks. After that, she called me by my real and forever name, Arthur.

I am so relieved that I made it past all the changes without an identity crisis. I remained the working guy who I have always been despite what name I was called at the time. I am Arthur Dogson Todd. If I know you, it's okay to call me "Arthur."

The sound of my name and the way O'mamma holds on to each part when she calls me for a job makes me feel special. "Arrr-thurr!" It's also the name of a long-ago king. I bet his mother called him that same way when she needed his help, "Arrr-thurr!"

King Arthur grew up to be a hero. He was in charge of the protection of more land than I ever will see. I'm trying to live up to his name, and mine.

Misty Meadows is what O'mamma eventually called our farm. The story is that when she and Mr. Cliff first moved out here, there was she still likes to say, "a beautiful fall mist drifting over the newly cut pastures on the hill early each morning." To O'mamma, it was a magical sight. She thought about the names Magical High Meadow and High Meadow Mist.

Mr. Cliff got "sit-down serious" with her and told her to pull up a chair. "Listen carefully," he said. "Those names for a farm might be misunderstood in a state where the largest cash crop is illegal, and then our fields might be seized."

She didn't like his opinion, but she was scared enough to choose a name she thought was safer, Misty Meadows. Lately, she's been talking about calling our place something else.

O'mamma and Mr. C. had been enjoying a story about a huge abbey downtown. It arrived in the mail almost every day. I heard her say to her friends Caron and Dan that they saw four years of episodes in two months.

I didn't know how that worked, but they spent night after night in the living room watching it. The next day he'd bring it to the post office in its white and red paper wrapping.

After that routine got started, our entire schedule changed. We didn't even eat on time. Both became sapiens Pristine and I had never seen before. Sometimes, they stayed up so late that we went to bed long before they did.

They laughed, and they cried. During the day they talked about the sapiens' problems in the story or "What's gonna happen next?" That's all they cared about.

Mr. Cliff didn't show it, but we sensed he was more worried than she was. Then, one night in the dark, I heard him whisper, "O', are we addicted?"

It was hard on Pristine and me. We missed them, the ones we used to know.

"*What is going on, and where is this Abbey!*" we asked one another. I said, "*It can't really be downtown because it's in the country somewhere. It's probably not too far from here since O'mamma talks about wanting to visit.*" My guess was that it's at Leiper's Fork or in Dog Hollow near Fly.

O'mamma found out that her friend Nancy Healer had seen the same story. She "loved the look" of the Abbey, so she re-decorated her own house. O'mamma called the result "classically elegant."

Now Nancy wanted to help us turn our simple farmhouse into a "manorly" home. She laughed and said, "Finally, you will become mannerly people." I laughed too, *Ha! Ha!* like I knew what was funny about that.

They all seemed to have forgotten that the beautiful red and gold sign out front said Misty Meadows. I was happy when I remembered it was made of iron because iron is very, very heavy. So, if they had to dig it up and carry it to metal recycling, they might have to change their minds. I was still afraid the name of our place might become Misty Manor.

Suddenly and without any warning, there was a lot of rushing around and loud talking. Nancy had arrived. Our home became a work site. She and O'mamma ran from room to room taking things down off the walls.

Every new idea they shared ended with a cheer. They showed one another their favorite colors in a book and argued about which one was "the best for that spot." Most of our furniture was moved a few inches to the side or even to another room. Then, they'd change their minds and put it back where it had been in the first place.

Pristine and I stayed concerned as O'mamma and Nancy rushed past us talking fast, laughing loud, and breathing hard. They were working, working, working to make our comfy home into a "smaller bigger place" if I remembered the words in the right order.

We learned a new word from Mr. Cliff, "maniac." He was concerned too.

The madness threatened my job performance. Canine couches were shoved into out of the way places without considering how hard it would be to guard from under the bed or from behind the drapes. Nancy talked about moving "the staff" downstairs until O'mamma told her that "downstairs" here is just dirt, rock, and a dehumidifier.

"Listen to yourselves, sapiens. What has happened to your wisdom? I am a beautiful part of this family. You used to photograph me for our Christmas cards. I should not be relegated to guarding from behind the drapes. What has taken you over?

"Besides my good looks, you are losing your only protection from intruders. You need me!"

In a louder and deeper tone of voice, I said, *"I demand my place by the front door back. Give me my guarding post back or I will not guard!"*

I had worked myself into a temper tantrum, but it was ignored, so I made a strategic retreat. If I couldn't get their attention now, I decided that I would wait for a better moment.

It was comforting to listen to myself say, *"Time is on my side so I'm going to calm down, hang on to my self-worth, and chant a mantra while the madness unfolds.*

I'm counting on Mr. Cliff to come through like the hero she used to want him to be."

Last night he told her, "We cannot make Misty Meadows Farm into an abbey no matter what we do."

O'mamma stood up and paced back and forth in front of him. "Think more positively like the little engine that could," she replied.

That made no sense since engines slept until you turned them on, and then their noise was so loud that nobody could think. And which one was she talking about anyway, the lawnmower? She might have meant his tractor, but no one would have dared to call his Kubota L430 a "little" engine.

Over and over again O'mamma said, "If you try and I try and if you believe and I believe, we can reach our goal."

Finally, she shouted, "Yes We Can! One day we will become Misty Manor!"

They both looked exhausted. We all went to bed at the same time.

Part 2: The Incremental Person

The next morning I was outside in the sun near the mudroom door. O'mamma playfully calls this part of my work "sun-guarding." I was relaxed until she began speaking like someone on a mission to convince or die trying.

"Uh, oh! It's not over yet," I thought.

In the kitchen, she was going on a rant about the benefits of being incremental to get to the faraway goal of creating Misty Manor Abbey. She was telling him to be an Incremental Person, but she said it without actually saying it.

Mr. Cliff knows his stuff. He didn't get confused. He got quiet, listened to what she said, and didn't ask questions.

In my comfy position on the pavers, I was wondering, *"What is an incremental person?"* He'd never ask. I knew he'd never ask. She knew it too.

Without waiting for the question, she answered it, "An incremental person does things little by little, bit by bit, all the while having great faith that the little bits will make something big.

"An incremental person patiently enjoys the challenge of each bit. He does not constantly look at how much more there is to do. He becomes a positive force for the good of all." She had told him how to be her hero.

His head twitched slightly. He shifted in his chair. I imagined that the words "enjoys the challenge" and "patient" had gotten to him. But my guy didn't move a muscle or blink an eye.

So often, Mr. Cliff could predict what she'd say, so he sat quietly guessing at what would come next. He prepared himself to be asked why he didn't care about her dream and why he wouldn't love to live in a place like the Abbey.

I wondered if he was hoping for criticism because then he could justify crying out "Unfair!" and end the conversation. That did not happen.

O'mamma made a sideways move and switched the focus. *"O Big Brown Short-Haired Dog! She is going to use me as an example again. Yup, Pup, there she goes."*

"Take Arthur, for example, he worked minute by minute, and it added up to hours and hours of guarding. The wonderful result is that we have an alarm system built by his steady bit-by-bit contribution. We need to continue to live by the standard Arthur has set."

This conversation might have bad consequences for me. It's a fact that guys are suspicious of other guys who try to look extra good to women. We watch each other looking for holes in their holiness. Even the rooster used to cock-a-doodle-do in a lower than normal, more masculine tone when O'mamma was outside. I know how to suspect a guy going in the wrong direction.

I hoped this didn't make Mr. C. suspicious of me. Did he know I fell asleep on the job sometimes? I bet he did. If he knew, would he use it? How jealous was he? Were there photos? Would they dim the glow of my reputation?

Fear had made my racing mind lose control of all rational thoughts. I stopped myself and pretended I was listening to O'mamma's voice saying, "Calm down. Take your fears one by one. Be an incremental worrier!"

"*Okay, I will,*" *I said.*

"First, no one is perfect. I'm not, and neither are sapiens, not even heroes and not even Presidents.

"So, if the way their reputations glow isn't dimmed by the big, bad things they do, with only minor flaws mine won't be either."

I stated my position with a slow, resolute groan, "*I was voted into this family, and I will not be forced out!*"

I realized I might be overreacting, but that didn't matter. I was worn out and didn't consider myself strong enough to make it through the next worry. So, I told myself that anything I did, even take a nap, counted as an increment.

ABOUT BEING RIGHT

P rotection is my forever profession. It brings out my best qualities, so I like to say I was born to do it. I need to focus on being right to make life-saving decisions, but there is more to it than that. I also need my sapiens to be right about me, who I am, how hard I work, and what I stand for.

Guarding is the most valuable service I can give them. It isn't as easy as it may look to casual observers watching the protector lying on a bed with his eyes closed. The demands of the job truly are underestimated. Even though no one else might consider it to be as stressful as air traffic control, it has come close to that level for me.

I operate out of several guarding stations. Each one has been chosen for its maximum range of surveillance coverage. All that's needed is enough quiet to hear the sounds of predators in the area.

Squirrel static used to be a major problem. I listened carefully until I got to know the sounds of their language. Trying to decipher their chatter, I made a lot of practice runs at those guys to see what they'd say. It turned out they talked about nuts and trees and holes in the ground, nothing important for my job protecting Misty Meadows Farm. We became friends, but for the sake of efficiency I learned to tune them out.

Different times of day bring different types of intrusion. Hour by hour, I move to the workstation nearest the location of the most likely threat. I won't deny that I consider how comfortable a station is as I choose my position. In fact, comfort does get a lot of weight so much that I developed a Comfort Level Rating System, the CLRS.

At First Level stations (ComfLev1) I'm guarding inside or outside on a bed or on soft grass in a sunny area, no twigs or rocks underneath. Stations considered Second Level (ComfLev2) have grass and sun with a few pebbles and some wind allowed. Third Level (ComfLev3), not often selected, is with no sun, on bare dirt, small roots and rocks allowed, but no ant hills. Not yet, nor about to be selected, is Fourth Level on gravel.

Use of the CLRS would be approved by the Canine Guarding Association, I'm sure, if I sent them the guidelines. They must already recognize as a fact that the level of concentration for all professionals is directly proportional to their level of mental and physical comfort.

In other words, if the best guarding a dog can do depends on how well he concentrates, then the obvious conclusion is that dogs must be as comfortable as possible on the job.

What happened this morning shows a lot about the typical response to an intruder-alert. As usual, around 10:30 a.m., I was guarding from the family bed upstairs.

At 10:35, to be precise, from a ComfLev1 position, I sensed that our northeastern perimeter had been crossed by a vehicle. I gave the Fair-Warning Bark, signaling that this property was patrolled. That way the intruder had a chance to retreat, and I wouldn't have left my post unnecessarily. With no sign that this situation had ended on its own, I rushed down the back stairs barking the Intruder-Alert Bark. O'mamma recognized the deep tone and opened the back door.

The same old doubting and dissension from Mr. Cliff followed me from the kitchen, through the mudroom, and into the yard. He was drinking coffee and saying, "Relax, Arthur. Go back to bed. No one is out there."

"That's not helpful, Mr. C!" I gave him the squinchy-eye without missing a step. I knew he probably would not get the message because his eyes are usually closed as he sips.

More confident in my keen senses, O'mamma always looks outside when I bark that bark. If she doesn't see anything, she always tells him, "Arthur is always right." "Always, always, always" boosts my ego, but in the midst of the crisis, I can't afford to pause to enjoy it.

"Let's face facts, Mr. C. As the one protecting Misty Meadows 24-7 for years, I've had more opportunities to be right than you have."

I would never bring it up, but I do wonder if he would trade places with me if it were physically possible. That is the biggest secret thought I have ever had. It goes along with my secret suspicion that Mr. Cliff has been jealous of the admiration I get from O'mamma about the many successes I've enjoyed.

It wouldn't be the right thing to do, but this is what I'd like to say. *"Get a grip man. We aren't in a competition. This is my job. I'm the one with the canine ears and nose. I'm supposed to be right about these things, and it hasn't always been easy.*

"Rightness is an art, an art and a discipline that develops over time. Being Young and Right is riskier than being Old and Right because together Young and Right are downright Cocky and Arrogant. I discovered that when the pair brought me nothing but combat."

Through a lot of suffering early in my life, I've become an expert on the subject of addiction to Rightness. When I was younger, I wasn't mature enough to be careful, cautious, strategic, and so on, like I am now. I had a lot of energy and very little patience. The worst part was that I tried to be right about anything and everything, all the time.

I was unbearably bossy. No one was spared my superior attitude when I was cock-sure I was making sense. I'm ashamed to say it now, but some called me "obnoxious," and I didn't even care. All I cared about was being right. For years it was my only goal.

The narrowness of that mindset set me back. I was such a failure I couldn't keep my tail curled and held high. I suffered humiliation and scary dreams from pulling so many false alarms and bogus predictions. The pain of sneers and jeers, proof of my unpopularity, forced me to review my ways.

I made the crucial decision to become cautious about when, where, and why I got involved in being right. I promised myself I'd gather information for important problems only. Sounds, smells, and suspicions that could lead me to success in saving property and lives would have to become my only focus.

The first thing I gave up was trying to regulate the daily problems the hens had with each other. I told them I was through.

"It doesn't matter who is right. Get in line, girls. Be fair to each other and take turns. I'm sorry, but who gets on the nest first is not a matter of loss of life or property. Canine wisdom cannot be wasted on who is next to lay an egg."

From then on, the only worthy reason to be right was to excel in my profession—protection!

The adventure this morning proved that my growth hasn't stopped just because I have overcome so much of who I used to be.

O'mamma rushed outside after me. Together we approached the northeastern perimeter. We saw that the intruder was only Builder Doug. My job of guarding was done, but I stayed out of curiosity. I told myself, *"This is an off-the-job opportunity to watch sapiens behave in their mysterious ways."*

Builder Doug looked stressed. *"Why?"* I asked myself.

"Don't ask questions! Observe only! There is nothing to figure out and nothing to be right about. You're not working... he is.

"Okay." I agreed with my advice and sat on the grass near O'mamma. Still, it was hard to relax. Before I could begin a mantra, our builder's face and neck turned red.

The problem he struggled with looked unusual. He was attacking his own truck. The white truck he drove wouldn't let him in.

"I need a strong, metal hanger," he said gruffly to O'mamma. She rushed to find one. In three blinks of an eye, she handed him the strongest one she had. He jabbed and poked until the truck gave in and let him open the doors.

Yup, pup! It happened without my help. I didn't need to know anything or be right about anything. I never imagined it could be so easy.

I felt so free! As I breathed out a long sigh, I realized I hadn't even needed to chant a mantra. With just a minor mental adjustment in a matter of seconds,

I was on vacation from *rightness* in a relaxed and happy place.

On my way upstairs to a late morning ComfLev1 guarding post, I heard O'mamma say, "Arthur was right. Admit it. He's always right when he's guarding." As usual, Mr. C. did not reply.

Let them toss me back and forth like a ball in their little game. Sapiens have a way of looking like they're serious even if they aren't. I hoped it was only a game. I couldn't tell, so I let it go.

When I'm not under the stress of Precise Performance, "Always, Always, Always" is my favorite song.

"Don't-Always-Need-To-Be-Right" Mantras

(to be chanted rhythmically)

STRONG

I'm a canine
Right or wrong.
Doesn't matter
'Cuz I'm strong.
Strong when I'm right,
Strong when I'm wrong,
Strong, strong,
Right or wrong.

LET-IT-GO

Let it go, Let it go.
Let it go, go, go
If it's not my business,
It can go... go... go.

THE MYSTERY OF THE MISSING EGGS

Part 1: The Suspect Suffers

When you're feeling great about yourself, nothing is more upsetting than your own family casting looks your way, suspicious looks. All you can do is quietly wait for the charges to be stated.

"You are a suspect in an ongoing egg theft case." I knew at any minute that's what could be thrown my way.

I decided that denial would be my first reaction. I needed to be prepared, so I practiced. *"Not me! I'm not a thief! These charges are totally unfounded. The evidence is based on it on your 'trusted' memories of me when I was a puppy.*

"I've overheard you talking. I don't sleep as much as you think I do. Show me proof from other witnesses. Let the facts speak. They will tell the truth."

When I was young, everything was new to me. I discovered things faster than I was able to understand what they were about. And while I happily jumped from one bit of excitement to another, I was being observed kindly I assumed at the time. I thought my puppyhood was great. If I had a "record," I didn't know it.

When they chose to adopt me, O'mamma and Mr. Cliff hadn't lived with a puppy in ten years. That must have been the reason why so often they didn't understand what they saw.

"Look at R.T.! He's so cute! Oh, no! He's trying to get the cat!"

"Not true. This is what puppies and cats do. This is how we play. I like to run and the cat does too. What would I do with her if I caught her?"

I didn't know. They didn't either.

"Look at R.T.! He's trying to make the tortoise pull his head back in."

"Am I? Maybe I'm having fun rolling him over with my nose. Maybe he has a fascinating scent."

I didn't know. They didn't either. I wasn't planning. I was playing.

There's a whole list of what they saw me do. O'mamma wrote a lot of it in words on paper. She took a few photos of me, but not many. *"Hmm... there are a lot of words, and only a few pictures. Hmm... was it part of a plan?"*

Maybe the reason was O'mamma and Mr. Cliff had already captured enough images of what they called "fur on four." Other canines had joined the family, some before me. Panda was a pup, and Kenya, Sparkle Plenty, and Pristine came as adults. There were lots of pictures in albums still standing on the bookshelf near the kitchen.

So when the reason for no proof in pictures turned out to be neglect and not a plan, did that make me feel better? No, it didn't.

The big problem was what had happened back then wasn't staying back then. It seemed like their minds continued to go to the past while they were trying to solve a present-day egg theft mystery. And probably the only evidence possible would come from old memories of unnamed "witnesses."

I asked myself, *"If I think there is no solid evidence, why do I feel so bad? Let me say it this way. I am upset, but the evidence doesn't upset me. I try to question myself, but I don't make sense.*

"Am I asking the right question? A better one might be this. What makes me believe there is a charge of egg theft hanging over me?" I did have answers for that.

Suspicious looks coming from O'mamma were the first thing that came to mind. Looks didn't count as proof, but I got strong feelings from them. "Guilty!" The looks were talking to me. "You are guilty of egg theft!" they said.

I was hearing in words what the looks were making me feel. *"Well, that's easy to fight,"* I thought. *"I'll just talk back to the feelings that hit my heart hard. I'll say, 'You want me to feel bad over something that's not true.*

I'm not buying it! Ha!'" I wondered if it would be that simple.

I needed a new mantra, but there wasn't time.

Hints of suspicions continued to come and go, so I put the new strategy into action. When O'mamma said, "We're not getting as many eggs as a month ago," I read her glance and detected an insulted feeling inside. I fought back with my own words. When Mr. Cliff said, "Are the hens molting? The big girl is missing some tail feathers." I talked back sharply and then relaxed by inhaling and closing my eyes.

Then, O'mamma answered him with "No, they don't lay eggs when they're molting," and the trust I felt said my sapiens didn't think I was the thief. Surprisingly, now I could expect feelings to tell me something good as well as bad. That was good! But the next day, words of suspicion, anger, and insult jumped back in and tore at my heart again.

O'mamma returned from the barn and reported that one brown egg was missing from the nest. Being extra precise, she described the scene. A brown egg had been lying next to three pale ones and now the brown one was gone. She eyed me. I knew what she was remembering.

Part 2: The Prior Protection Program

W ay back, we had lots of hens... ten, twenty, or thirty at a time. The hens laid eggs everywhere, and babies popped up out of broken eggshells in the nest or on the ground. Tiny little fuzzy things peeked out at me from under their mothers' wings.

My rival the rooster was their father. I knew that but when they looked at me as I wandered around, I got a soft feeling like a father has when he looks at his pups.

At the time everyone had begun talking about being "in harm's way." I caught on to that concept fast, but there's a gap between understanding an idea and having a method. I hadn't prepared a plan for when danger got here.

An entire fox family invaded the yard. Only the rooster and I were on duty. I panicked and ran. The rooster fought off the main guy and lost lots of feathers. He also lost six wives. It was awful.

The next time danger came. O'mamma was on the sun porch. Through the window, she caught sight of a lone fox forcing a hen to run round and round into smaller and smaller circles against the fence. The fox was ready to carry off the hen and eat her.

O'mamma screamed my name. "Arr-thurr! Get down here!"

Upstairs at my most comfortable guarding post, I couldn't rouse a fighting spirit. I hadn't yet become my warrior self. The truth was that I was afraid to engage without knowing if I'd win, and the feeling of Direct Mouth Capture was still a vivid memory.

I didn't actually see what happened with my own eyes, but I pictured the scene as I listened to Mr. Cliff describe it. O'mamma ran outside toward the fox with the kitchen broom swinging it wildly and screaming her ear-piercing scream. "He stood there defiantly," she said, "as if he owned our place."

Was it was her screaming or the broom she swung at him that made him turn tail and run? She tells the story with an unlikely explanation at the end. "With a broom, no makeup, unkempt hair from the wind, and a black shirt on, he thought I was a witch!"

A stronger possibility was that after she called my name, he knew I'd be on my way down the stairs in a blink. No one will ever know, so the proof of his fear of me will be a forever mystery.

After that, I tried to take action before danger came. I decided to start up the *Prior Protection Program*. (PPP) If a sense of danger floated over like a threatening storm cloud, I'd pick up a baby chick gently and carry it to a safer place like nearer to its mother. I glanced at the house as I worked and basked in the imagined praise coming my way for being dedicated to the welfare of poultry.

Sometimes eggs didn't look safe where they were outside on the ground. Carefully holding my jaws steady in a precise position, I'd moved them one at a time to a nest or other safe place. I even buried a few in case the rest might be stolen or broken. I knew I was still being observed, but for some reason, the praise didn't come through as clearly as before.

Then an egg broke while I was carrying it. When I stepped into a hole and twisted my leg, my jaw clenched and cracked the shell. For the first time, I had to clean up a broken egg. I licked my lips and smiled. Wow! The taste of a fresh egg thrilled me!

I paused to review the entire scope of the job I was doing for the hens. Feeling proud, I told myself, *"This is a real job. I began at the bottom as an unpaid worker, a volunteer for the greater good. Now I'm in charge of the Prior Protection Program. I even have a side benefit, a perk for a job well-done, cleaning up if there's an accident."*

I became more and more aware that an egg might break at any moment. The excitement kept my tail wagging. What was my real job—protecting or cleaning up a tasty egg? I suspected a shift toward self-interest.

"Am I trying to help the chickens and just them? Am I hoping in my helping that I will break an egg and be forced to do the cleanup? Have I stumbled into self-deceit and temptation?"

Before I could find the answers on my own, Mr. Cliff gave me the cure for temptation. At dinner, he looked down and tilted his head back and stared sideways at me. Then he declared loudly to all in the room that in the Great Depression when he was a boy "egg-suckin' dawgs" disappeared in the night. "That's how farmers in Tennessee used to talk back then," he said with a frown.

He liked to tease, so at first, I thought he was playing. But then, I realized there could be traces of egg left on my whiskers. That yellow part sticks like glue. *"Was it there? Had he noticed?"* I panicked.

It was both Fear-of-Death and Fear-of-Humiliation that suddenly gripped me. No self-respecting canine would want to be called "an egg-suckin' dawg" or be threatened with disappearing in the night over the taste of a fresh egg. He could have been playing, but I couldn't risk being helpful any longer.

The time had come to choose between what was best for poultry and what was best for me. At that very moment, I turned over the survival of the species to Mother Nature and my pride in my perks to my conscience.

Temptation was dead. Without any internal conflict, my chest relaxed, and as a result I was able to hold my head a little higher.

In the meantime, I was still a suspect in the ongoing egg theft case, but my suffering was less now that my conscience agreed with my decision.

Part 3: X-Terminator Arrives

All of a sudden O'mamma ran from the old barn to the house. *"Wait a minute,"* I thought, *"she's not a sudden kind of person."* Sure, she can react fast like she did when Pristine and I were roughing up the groundhog. But this looked alarming, so I followed her inside.

She began telling Mr. Cliff about a snake that was as long as the old, white door that's lying on its side in the barn. "It has dark diamonds on its back," she said. "Maybe it's a rattler." She wanted him to get the gun and come outside.

Pristine and I moved to the other side of the room and listened closely.

Mr. Cliff isn't a sudden kind of person either. He's more of a "there, there, nothing to worry about, little lady" kind of guy. Usually, that doesn't work for her, but she did seem to relax when he said it was a rat snake and not a rattler.

O'mamma went to the computer and entered "rat snakes in Tennessee." Sure enough, there was a photo of the snake she had seen in the barn. I hadn't noticed anyone out here with a camera, but he was all rounded up like a hosepipe with dark diamonds on his back right there on the screen in front of her.

"How did he get past me to the computer?" I wondered.

Of all the things she might have done at the sight of him, she named him! "I'm going to call him X-Terminator." Wow! I didn't see that coming. Really slowly she said, "X-Ter-min-a-tor," like she was thinking that it's really nor-mal to give a snake a name.

I don't care how special his name sounds or how slowly you say it. The important thing is... he's a snake. *"Just call him Snake,"* I said. *"That tells all anyone needs to know."* Supposedly, he eats rats, but I don't accept any of his qua-li-fi-ca-tions. I just can't.

Do you know how fast rats run? Even if you tried to see one running, he would be gone before you did. You can't turn your head quickly enough to follow them with your eyes. The trick is to stare straight ahead and let them all go by. If three run past, you might see one. Despite their proven speed, Snake, with no legs, feet, toes, or toenails, has claimed to be faster.

"Show me," I shouted in anger at their admiration for someone who didn't deserve it.

Pristine is a rat terrier, bred to catch rats. She has never caught any. When there were packs of them running through the old barn, she had her choice of which to chase. She couldn't catch even the slowest one. Being a rat terrier who can move fast enough to keep up with a quarter horse on smooth ground while running uphill and barking didn't help her to be fast enough to do the job.

A fact about rats is that they don't see well in bright sunshine, so a few times O'mamma tried to help Pristine by putting the chicken feed outside the coop on the grass in the sun. They had to "come and get it" if they wanted to eat.

Pristine did everything right... picked a good hunting spot, froze and barely breathed, didn't wag, stared straight ahead, and waited. When the rats came outside for the food, she ran at them every time following them into the barn and jumping up trying to nab one.

Pristine had worked hard at being the best rat terrier she could be for a solid week. Then it rained, and she gave up. I was so busy with squirrel chasing that I didn't have time to help her. Honestly, I'm better having an assistant than being one, anyway.

Not to brag here, but I actually did run fast enough to catch a squirrel on my own when I was a little younger and thinner. I let the little guy go before I gagged that time.

Part of Snake's fantastic reputation was that he ate rats without regular teeth like we have. Supposedly, he swallowed them whole. That couldn't be true either. Those rats had gotten fat eating the hen's corn and Laying Formula. He wouldn't have been able to open his mouth wide enough to get one in. Besides that, he wasn't round enough for it to go all the way through. It was all a ridiculous lie!

He might have eaten the rats while the rats were eating the eggs. If that was true, I bet the rats didn't want to let Snake have their eggs. They must have taken too long deciding whether to keep eating or to run. So, conveniently, he was able to nab them while they hesitated.

All the rats disappeared, but I don't believe he can take credit for eating every one. Who knows? It's possible he just smells bad, and they left on their own. I know I couldn't live with a possum in the house. I'd move out.

I was convinced Snake was the one eating our eggs. *"Think about it. No running was required. Eggs lie still waiting to be picked up. Instead of step by step, he got to them slither by slither."*

Part 4: Exonerated

A round the time when I was mistakenly and unfairly suspected of the crime of egg theft, I tried to make myself believe Snake just happened to show up at the old barn. But coincidences never made sense. I believe everything is connected to everything else, and most of everything else is connected to you.

Mr. Cliff called that idea "paranoia," so I told him, *"Nothing just happens. Things happen for a reason. If you think really hard and long and don't give up, you will discover something in your mind that can prove everything is connected to everything else."* He scowled and walked away. He knew O'mamma believed me.

She says we are all connected to someone called Mother Nature, especially when we are outdoors. Supposedly, she's a force who was put in charge of everything that sapiens didn't have control over yet. A lot of sapiens think she follows rules that aren't fair, but they want it to rain on the lawn and not on the picnic.

Mother Nature ends up being criticized for not listening. If what they want doesn't happen, they don't stop to think that everyone is asking for something different at the same time. Her clouds and temperature can't work that way. Even I can't patrol along the park fence and guard the hens at the same time.

On television, teams of weather-sapiens guess at what she'll do next so everyone will know what to wear or when to find a safe place to hide when she wreaks havoc. Sometimes what she does is awful. Once in a while, she fools us and does something great that wasn't in the forecast. I think we should thank her for unpredicted beautiful days and do something nice for her Earth. That might make her feel good and help her to stop doing some of the terrible things she does.

If fire is harming birds and trees, they say Mother Nature's lightning started it. It can be true it was her lightning, but sometimes it turns out, sadly, the alcohol in someone and the fire he made caused the forest to burn.

There's a guy Mr. Cliff knows he calls "Sorry," but I don't think that's his real name. When he has alcohol in him, he doesn't go camping. He drives his truck and crashes into mailboxes on our road. Mr. Cliff says both bad behavior and alcohol are responsible for a lot of destruction.

"Is bad behavior a force of nature?" I asked. Mr. Cliff said, "No, Mother N has no power over that!"

O'mamma has never been comfortable being the "little lady who shouldn't worry." So naturally, she spent a lot more time on the computer checking for information about her new farm worker I call Snake. After all, she knew nothing about his history.

He had arrived uninvited with no papers to show where he was from and to prove he wasn't dangerous to us who already worked here. Pristine and I and the cats and horses all came with papers. Actually, Mr. Cliff and O'mamma showed papers when they got married.

Suddenly, there was shouting from the chat room. Without anyone expecting it to be over so soon, her worry and the computer had combined forces to bring about the ending with one click of the mouse. She had the answer to the mystery!

O'mamma had been gazing at the screen a long time. All of a sudden, a look of shock came over her. She clicked to look at a photo. Then she jumped up with her right fist in the air shouting, "SNAKES EAT EGGS."

In a blink, I was cleared of egg theft. Just three words had set me free. How did I react? I don't remember. I do know she looked at me. She smiled and slowly said, "Snakes... eat... eggs. The mystery is solved, Arthur."

I remember saying it to myself again and again. *"Snakes eat eggs. Snakes eat eggs."*

Zap! I was declared innocent! It happened so fast that it startled me. My heart was pounding. Then I fell into a pit of *Mightily Angry Madness (MAM)*.

"That snake has been the cause of my pain and suffering for weeks." I couldn't get away from that thought. I was still in the pit suffering but not with fear. It was rage! I hated him with all my strength.

Soon, I began to feel sorry for myself. None of this would have happened if he had never come to Misty Meadows or if my sapiens had trusted me and accepted my opinion. I'd been right from the get-go. A snake is a snake is a snake is a snake. Sadly, no one had listened. There was no use in looking back.

O'mamma didn't notice my distress. She was too excited about solving the mystery. She ran out to the coop. I followed slowly, tail flagging. Like a detective, she looked for evidence, anything that would prove Snake had been the real thief.

The evidence was obvious, grooves in the sand five inches wide and very long in front of the chicken wire door to the hen pen where eggs wait to be picked up. He had slithered across the very spot we were standing on.

Amazing! We stood there in silence for a moment with heads bowed and stared.

O'mamma got a bunch of three-foot-long hay bale twine and rubbed the strings together between her thumb and fingers. "Like the Natives did to keep snakes away when they lived here, I'm putting rows of the frayed twine across his path to the nests. Snakes don't like to cross fuzzy twine, so really it's a fuzzy fence," she said.

I knew she was attempting to convince herself it would work. If it would turn out she was right, all her worrying about the eggs being in danger could come to an end.

I was still struggling to get over the fact that he had preyed on me as well as stolen eggs. His presence had been so powerfully hurtful that it was hard to accept without question that a few pieces of string would stop him.

"Why won't she give in to the idea that snakes don't behave according to anything that makes common sense? Snakes' ways go against everything normal when they eat without teeth and move without legs. Why say a snake will never cross a fence made of string?"

I admire O'mamma, but I refuse to accept her fuzzy-fence theory. Sapiens seem to want to control everything, but how will they ever do that if what they base their decisions on doesn't make sense? *Sigh...*

I am sure of one thing. Snake's mistake of lying along the door in the old barn where O'mamma would notice him was not, not, not a coincidence. Everything is connected to everything else. Even if it is what Mr. Cliff calls "paranoia," it works for me.

We came back inside. O'mamma sat down on the rug next to me and stroked my face and ears gently. She looked into my eyes and said, "It's over, Arthur. I'm sorry you suffered." I sighed... *"It's going to take a while."*

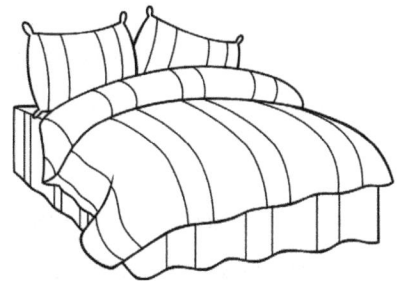

THE UNCERTAIN WITNESS

C o-bedding is a wonderful kind of togetherness for the four of us. Every night we sleep in our special places. Mr. Cliff is on the side by the door with a lot of space around him. He's a thrasher. I'm on the other side by O'mamma's feet, and Pristine is next to her knees.

We get under the covers when it's cold, but we never ever put our heads on the pillows. They're only for our sapiens. That's a part of Proper Bediquette, the unwritten list of rules we follow to keep us considerate of others in bed.

I've noticed that we're happier if we follow rules than if we don't. Usually, I can tell ahead of time which kind of unhappiness breaking a particular one will bring. In the case of the Not My Pillow rule, it's hard to imagine, but it might be something about discomfort.

It could be about whiskers tickling bare skin, or maybe our wet noses are the problem. Maybe it's just something ordinary, but unwelcome, like snoring or air that's not fresh because one of us has already breathed it.

Since I sleep at the foot of the bed, the rule doesn't matter to me, anyway. I never thought much about it until last night.

Halfway between dark and dawn, Pristine made a Bad Bediquette move. I had been kicking off the comforter because I was too hot when I saw her make a run for the top. Actually, she crawled slowly up to the pillow where she rested her head right next to O'mamma's.

There they lay, a princess and her queen, nose to nose on the same pillow. Since it had never happened before, I was fearful. Situations like this, unexpected rule violations, put us in danger of being unhappy.

What was my girl thinking? Maybe she was lost in a dream. I pictured a child's mother reading from a story in a book, "Princess Pristine was lying on the pillow dreaming, unaware she had made a forbidden move against her Queen." That sounded better than it looked, forgivable and all. Once in a while, she does seem a little like a princess, especially when she wears pink and does her Nose-Up-Walk.

It's possible she hasn't been with us long enough to realize that there are rules for good reasons. Then again, we've seen her do whatever feels good at the moment instead of doing what O'mamma just asked her to do.

Now that I'm thinking more deeply about it, Pristine has never worried about things I consider serious. She's more of a free spirit untroubled by deep thought, oblivious and, therefore, fearless.

The bedroom was quiet for a while. Then O'mamma began mumbling like she was dreaming. Her eyes opened. Her nose grazed Pristine's as she sat straight up. She was rubbing her cheeks and shaking her head like someone saying "no." Had Pristine's whiskers tickled O'mamma?

Suddenly, the room felt chilly. O'mamma said something startling, something no one would ever expect to come from her. It was hard to be sure. If I heard right and if I wasn't dreaming, I think she shouted, "You are not my equal!"

Then she fell back on the pillow, and her eyes closed. The room was quiet again. Mr. Cliff gave no sign that he had heard anything.

My thoughts were racing. *"What did I just witness? Why did she say that?"* The woman in bed with us was not the one I thought I knew. It was her, but it wasn't. It was so startling that it was hard to stop the rapid flow of questions.

"What about the respect she shows us every day?

"What about the doors and gates she holds open until we go through and sharing food at every meal?"

"You are not my equal." Where did that come from, her dark side?

Mr. Cliff and O'mamma say hurtful words can come from there. And if you have a big dark side, you can cause serious harm to the ones you love. They say, you have to promise to find out why it's there and fix it. Only then, can we trust you and like you again. And that's when we say we forgive you, and we make our hearts feel like it never happened.

I hope she doesn't have a big dark side. I hope she's who I thought she was. Even if she is, there might be another problem. What comes from that side even once can be a crime. If it is, whoever saw what happened is supposed to report it to the authorities.

That thought put me under pressure to remember exactly what I'd seen and heard. It had happened fast, as fast as three blinks. During cross-examination, witnesses can't answer quickly enough because their memories fail them. Their stories fall apart. They fall apart. Then they get attacked. They suffer.

I wanted to protect myself from that fate, so I thought back on each moment as it happened last night.

1. Pristine moved up to the pillow and put her nose next to O'mamma's nose.
2. I was the only witness.
3. O'mamma sounded like she was waking up from a dream.
4. She didn't look like herself.
5. She said something hurtful and unusual. "You are not my equal."
6. I could be wrong. Maybe she said, "You are not my angel."

7. She did not make Pristine move off the pillow.

8. No pillowcase was changed in the morning.

9. I could have dreamed all of it.

After the careful review, it was clear. The only victim in this incident was me. I asked myself, *"Should I try to explain what happened?"*

Who could I tell? Everyone we knew trusted O'mamma. No one would believe she has a dark side. Not a good idea! I could end up being called something upsetting and untrue, like a Canine Complainer begging for sympathy or worse than that—a Pathetic Paw Pointer!

Telling the truth has ruined a lot of good reputations, so I decided to protect mine.

DRIVEN TO DECEPTION

O n the days Big J works at our barn, he stops at the postbox at the end of the driveway on his way in. Yesterday, O'mamma's eyes popped open wide when he handed her the mail.

There on top of the pile was a large postcard with a full-color photo of a juicy hamburger, tomatoes and lettuce on a bun. Underneath was one word in large letters, "FREE." The newest brick box restaurant with the double sliding glass windows had addressed it to Resident, Misty Meadows Farm, Battle Station, TN.

Smiling as she picked up the card, O'mamma said, "Look at this! If I go to the new fast food place before it closes Sunday evening, I can get a free burger with the purchase of a drink. All I have to do is give a dollar and the coupon when someone opens the window to take my order. What a good deal!"

Then she lowered her head like something serious had come to mind. An upset look on her face took away her smile.

She rushed to call her best friend Harlow. "I have a predicament. This morning, I got a coupon in the mail for free food. Picture this scene with me, please, and tell me what you think."

"Okay, tell me," she said.

"At the window of the drive-through, I'll order a hamburger, give the girl the coupon, and pay for a drink. She'll come back with the food, and I'll speed away. Then the scrumptious smell will be filling the car. The more my mouth waters, the faster I'll drive. So I'll pull over, stop, and tear open the bag. It'll be gone before I get home."

"Sounds good, so what's the problem?" asked Harlow.

"So far, there isn't one, and there won't be until I'm near that place again. The next time I go past it, I already know how good their food tastes. My mouth will water, and I'll want some. So, can you see me there fighting with myself because I know I shouldn't stop? What if that happens every day?

"The problem is that if I sample this food even one time, I will never be free of wanting it. My freedom depends on not knowing how their burger tastes. What do you think? Am I over-reacting?"

The expression on O'mamma's face told me this was a serious matter, something with scary consequences. Harlow must have agreed because their conversation ended after that with the words, "Okay, that feels right. I'll do it now. Thanks!"

As soon as they hung up, she ripped up the postcard, coupon and all, into little pieces and let them drop directly into the recycling bin. I was startled, not only by her refusing food, free food, but also by the trap she feared.

"What was it about," I wondered. *"Are chefs who are actually wizards being hired to create recipes with secret, magic ingredients?*

"Are restaurants planning to catch more customers by capturing the taste buds of trusting sapiens and sell more burgers?

"Has O'mamma unwittingly uncovered the deception, Free for the Price of Freedom?"

I answered my own questions with three words. *"Yes, yes, and yes!"*

Before I witnessed O'mamma coming so close to the Free Burger Fate, I didn't know something so devious existed, and she didn't either. In a flash, it crossed my mind that it might happen to me, a canine.

I panicked when I realized it already had. I had succumbed to the Free Canine Biscuit Fate. I'd noticed unexplained longings that were making me restless and unhappy lately. And I was moping more than usual.

It was true! My freedom to choose what excited my own taste buds was being controlled. Nothing else satisfied my cravings except the canine biscuits given to dogs in cars at the bank. Would I have to continue to live in a state of constant deprivation unless I could get to the bank?

I thought back on the circumstances of how it began. Maybe I should have been alerted to something deceptive right away.

At O'mamma's bank, the window tellers had begun giving out free dog biscuits to canines in cars. I was suspicious. *"Why do that?"* I thought. *"Dogs don't have bank accounts."*

More suspicious than that was what they called them, "cookies." The wording wasn't right. Regular cookies are sweet. Biscuits are not. If it's a canine biscuit, why not call it that? You see what I mean! Why the switcheroo?

I wished I had stuck with my doubts instead of becoming enthralled by the taste of the first unexpected treat. I can't really blame myself.

When I look back, I realize that any canine would have been fooled and captured because we have the sharpest senses of all. What tastes good to other species tastes fabulously wonderful to us. We go to a level of enjoyment that should be considered nothing less than sublime.

The descent into my current compromised state had begun on the day I ate my first "cookie" at the bank. Around noon while I was lounging in the sun on the warm paved drive, O'mamma walked past me on her way to the car with checks in hand. "I have to go to the bank." The sweet, soft-eyed look she gave said, "You can come." Naturally, I hopped into the car, and we drove off.

With nothing in particular on my mind, I was relaxed, kind of mellow and feeling happy to be with her off the farm away from the others. As we pulled into the drive-through lane, I was lying in the front seat. O'mamma slipped her papers into the tube, placed it in the launcher, and pressed "Send."

The window in that brick box of a bank didn't slide open, yet a woman's voice came out somehow and said, "Would your doggy like a cookie?"

"Doggy?" I sat upright with ears perked looking for the owner of the voice. *"Who is she talking about? Me? I'm an adult. She should be talking like she's respectful of my dignity!"*

As a self-certified Canine Representative (CR), I am authorized to address her in the following manner. *"Your first mistake was the d**** word. You threw in a cutesy ending on the already marginally acceptable label and referred to me like I was some kind of baby. More than that, the word 'cookie' required that the second listed ingredient be sugar."* I knew how to sound official when I needed to.

I would have been satisfied if O'mamma had said, "His name is Arthur. He prefers to be addressed as the dignified canine he is, and yes, he would love a canine biscuit." But no, that didn't happen. O'mamma allowed the window teller to slide along in her narrow mindset, slipshod at best.

"Why would she miss an opportunity to educate?" I didn't know then, but I do know now. It's because sapiens were no longer allowed to attempt to expand anyone's mind without an invitation.

Offering an explanation of a new idea could lead to a word battle. If the recipient of new information ended up having a Bad Day, a recently passed law would have held the aggressor responsible for assault.

And if prior to his attempt at education, the aggressor had not stated words known to ward off that possibility, he could have been found guilty of assault with the intent to expand another party's mental awareness without written permission.

The Tennessee Annual Code has the crime described as "the willful and wanton disturbance of the right to be happy through vibes derived from socially acceptable and standardized interpersonal behavior." Sapiens are required to repeat the expected mantra, Have-a-Good-Day, or risk consequences.

Even though I was crushed and angry at having to let the matter go, I forced myself to overcome emotion, live in the moment, and enjoy the free biscuit. Immediately, the magic taste thrilled my buds, and all the distress was gone.

Whenever O'mamma went to the bank without me after that, I felt a new kind of bad. I lounged around and longed to forget the first time my taste buds had enjoyed the sublime. No matter what kind of good mood I might have had going on, the painful awareness I was missing out on the magic flavor of those treats hung like a dark cloud over me.

I hoped this new kind of bad feeling would never get to be the dangerously mad type of bad. I wouldn't want to get myself sent to a place where I never got another biscuit even from a visitor.

In those days of lying around with the longing, time crawled past my nose like a snail on its belly. To speed it up, I let my mind ride along with O'mamma in her car going south into the sunshine along Highway 31.

In my imagination, we were at the bank, and I was watching as the window teller gave biscuits to sapiens who showed up with a canine companion. I wanted a real biscuit so bad I could taste it. Thoughts of pleasure mixed with anger threw me into a swirl of confusion. My mood was deteriorating quickly.

To prevent the danger of impending rage, I took myself into a trance-like state. My eyes were reduced to squinting slits, and my brain made the switch to its dark side. From the deepest recesses of gray matter, I soothed myself with elaborate fantasies.

While I was gradually coming out of the trance, fantasy came closer and closer to becoming reality. No longer was I merely a bitter canine. I had evolved into an avenger with a plan to bankrupt the Bank.

The Plan: Manufacture Made in the USA Blow-Up Doggie Dolls for the passenger seats in cars, trucks, and SUV's. A strange pleasure filled my body with machine-like energy as I contemplated the details.

Multi-canine families could purchase several. Anyone could purchase several. There could be millions of "doggies" getting the free "cookies." Hoarders would come out in droves. Cookie bakers would smile at the ka-ching, ka-ching. Bankers would lose all of their money because their wizards' brilliant plan to deceive and capture was no match for my capabilities.

I'd make piles of money manufacturing dolls and even more selling "doggy cookie" storage containers hand painted to match car and truck colors. The manufacturing jobs created would solve the problem of unemployment.

The Medal of Freedom awarded by the President of the United States of America would be mine. Several years ago, I might have ended up as a guest at the State of the Union Address seated near Michelle. I used to dream about Bo and me romping in the Rose Garden. *"Too late now,"* I sighed...

A lot of effective plans have been based on deception. I'm not proud to say it, but this one was too. I'd never been dishonest in my life. In fact, puppies are not born capable of it, but they can be driven to deceive by cheaters' unfair practices because they to lose dignity when they lose free choice.

Bankrupting the Bank could lead to charges and a jury trial. I risked being found guilty of fraud, guilty of aiding and abetting fraudulent activity, and guilty of manufacturing paraphernalia for fraudulent purposes.

My defense would be if my mind had been captured as a prisoner in an economic war, it wasn't mine anymore so I was innocent. The jury would understand and decide that the Bank was at fault for my descent into criminal behavior.

I remembered something O'mamma has said many times. *"There is always the possibility of a bright side behind every dark side."* It was the same idea Mother Nature had when she put sunshine behind the clouds.

O'mamma and Mother Nature couldn't both be wrong, so I knew it was okay to hope for a good reputation again. Frantically, I made a list of what might have enough power to send my image at least halfway over to the acceptable side.

1. I could become known as an angry protester admired for my dark and clever ways while fighting for freedom from economic capture, a regular canine folk hero;

2. Someone could write a Bad-Boy Ballad to honor my success against the machine of the establishment;

3. I would write a book explaining the process of fighting deception with counter-deception; and

4. At the book signings, I would give out free canine biscuits to those who showed up with or without their canine companions.

The list itself was proof of my mind having been destabilized. An innocent pup could never have imagined those things.

If I carried out The Plan, I'd have to say goodbye to the life I have at Misty Meadows. Did I want to lead a destabilized life? Or did I want to forget the whole incident and return to guarding, my forever profession?

I thought about ComfLev1 mornings on the family bed and chasing squirrels and O'mamma's smile. It was easy to choose to go home.

Everyone needs to know my story. I won't keep it secret because messing with freedom is dangerous business. Many minds are at stake. I almost lost mine.

EVEN THE MOON HAS ANOTHER SIDE

Part 1: Awareness Arrives

O 'mamma's friends were calling me "sweet, lovable, and cute." Some women would let me sit on their laps while they talked with one another. A few allowed my head to rest on their chest pillows.

Men marveled at how many sapiens I had gathered as admirers. Both men and women were in awe of my finest attributes—wisdom, speed, and daring.

Just last week Big J wished the vet could reverse the very personal procedure I had at The Animal Hospital. He told Mr. Cliff he wanted me to give him a "chip off the old block," you know, a pup just like me. He must not have understood. It was more than a small incision. They're gone. I wish they were still mine. *Sigh...*

I was lap-sitting and casually wondering if women would enjoy being close if they knew I was dwelling on body parts when Awareness himself appeared in the form of a super-sized sapiens. Looming over me, he announced he had been sent to bring an important message. "The popularity you are enjoying is in danger of disappearing."

He informed me that I was harboring anger, jealousy, and excessive pride in a hidden Dark Side. Improper thoughts lived there too, he said, along with disdain, cowardice, and a superior attitude. I needed to pay attention or my world would crash down around me.

"It's not possible to keep all of that a secret forever," he warned. "Under pressure in a moment of emotional upset or even joyful exuberance, one or more of those things will be released. The other side of your otherwise wonderful self will be revealed, and the exposure will discourage sapiens from admiring you."

My brain was spinning on its stem. What had just happened? And where did he go?

Annoyed by the intrusion, I considered his message to be uninvited information, so I shook it off. Until I'd started enjoying the positive opinions of sapiens, I never had to keep track of what was in my mind. Thoughts came and went. No big deal. There wasn't anything in there I didn't know about.

Who was that guy? And who sent him? Nobody I knew.

A few hours later, I was listening to O'mamma review a few of her poems. *"I hope it'll be easy to make it through patiently,"* I thought. There are days when she can go over several versions of the same poem, changing only a word or two. But, there are others when she carefully examines each word erasing so many that there's hardly one left on the page. So far, I've done pretty well calming any irritation I detected.

One poem has a story that's extremely hard to bear. It's about Ohno the house cat she used to call her "baby" even though everybody knew that wasn't possible. What she wrote was unbelievable! It made him out to be so-o special. The truth was he tormented my girlfriend Sparkle Plenty and me.

Here's the proof...

INSIDE CAT

A cat prefers a cluttered house
Stacked with human stuff
A jungle of possessions where
Enough is not enough.

Paths through piles create terrain
With cover for a blind,
A necessity for hunters of the
Feline and the human kind.

Motionless along a limb,
His tree is just a chair.
Above the forest floor, he's poised
To pounce on travelers passing there.

With focused eye and open ear
He welcomes their blithe prance.
In their heart of hearts, they do believe
Their safety is not up to chance.

From jungle's unseen heights above
A flying leopard leaps and rides the backs
Of hapless dogs who thought their home
They had protected from attack.

A single bark was all it took to
End the siege and cause retreat.
The cat jumped up to a mountaintop
To sleep off his defeat.

I still don't see what could be cute about a cat jumping off the dining room chairs and riding our backs. How did she think he held on? Was he in a proper saddle? No. He held on with the equipment our so-called "friend" Mother Nature gave him, claws. I've always suspected O'mamma made it sound amusing so sapiens would admire her clever words.

A few other poems she wrote were about Mother Nature's beautiful gifts. Everyone knows that woman has been cruel to so many of us on Earth. O'mamma always leaves that part out. To her Mother Nature is only about beauty and change, color and form, and movement and rhythm. I think she almost worships the witch!

Yesterday while she was working, the side of me I had learned to ignore jumped out. O'mamma was examining a new poem very slowly. *"Oh-oh, gonna be one of those long days,"* I thought.

I tried to disregard the repeated chanting of her mantra that helped to banish unwanted words, "My-laser-saber-meant-to-sever-eliminates-the-extraneous."

None of it made sense because no scissors or swords were involved. All she had to work with was a pink eraser and a #2 yellow pencil. She questioned the presence of every word on the page and sucked my Reservoir of Patience dry as a dog bone in a drought.

The no-sense nature of it all was so upsetting I lost the last bit of self-control I had left. I wanted to strip off my fur coat and jump in the pond. I didn't, of course, but I couldn't hold back entirely. The nerve-jangling irritation came out in a horrendous howl.

Did I truly want to try holding back that side of me? I thought so, but the more often it happened, the worse I felt... no, actually... the better I felt.

The other side of the truth was that I enjoyed the powerful rush of feelings the howl brought even when it filled me with horrible distress. For a few precious moments, I'd have no thoughts, no worries, only pure, undiluted pleasure pouring from my inner being. I'd be left feeling limp and content until the fear and distress crept back in with my strength. Only because I lived with the fear of becoming a lost and lonely loser did I allow myself to rush back to the bright side every time.

Now that I'm brave enough to be completely honest, I confess the surge of pleasure propelled me to the edge of abandon. Once over and in, my spirit would soar to a new level of confidence.

I could stop and see myself like someone else would from afar. I was bad. Rocking side to side as I walked with a two-by-two-step swagger, the energy from being calm and cool lengthened my stride. A positively powerful canine was who I became.

Then, out of nowhere a suspicious thought flitted through my brain. My confidence took a dive. I stopped short and listened to my inner voice.

"You are being observed unkindly. Someone is laughing."

I could feel it!

"Oh, oh, here comes the Dark Si…" Wham! The switch to rage was instantaneous. I shouted, *"You Unaware Judgmentals have a Dark Side too!"*

Part 2: Delving into Darkness

In the Mental and Feelings Field where O'mamma works, she's helped many sapiens with what troubled them. I overheard her on the phone with someone yesterday.

"If you will bring all of yourself to a place where the parts you approve of and those you don't can live together, you will have a wonderful home to go to inside yourself. The energy you've fought against can become yours to use instead of being wasted."

"Was it possible she was right? Untroubled naps in a wonderful home? Awake with more energy?"

O'mamma continued. "Get to know what's trying to come from the other side of your nature. It's a part of you that wants to say something. Maybe it's about fear or anger or disappointment. Maybe you are still harboring memories of hurtful things.

"First, find a place with no distractions. Stay calm and think. Be aware of what you feel as you picture disturbing events from the past. Be sure to name each feeling.

"After you've watched the stories performed on a stage in your mind for a while, you'll know the dark parts so well you'll be prepared when they come back unexpectedly. Then, you'll have what you need, honest to goodness power to stay calm, think, and act in the way your entire self would want you to."

"Power! Yeah, but, she's talking about a lot of work and time. This could be tiring. I need a nap!"

Officially, I went on vacation from guarding. I needed enough time to face the old hurts and failures that were still hanging around in my mind. Why not begin with the ones that came back in bad dreams?

In the past when something unfair made me angry and I failed to assert myself or if I should have been aggressive and I wasn't, I'd be left with awful shame and regret. For one of those times, I've been able to create a new scene in my head that rights the wrong of what happened...

One spring morning at dawn, Pristine and I went out through the front doors. After a short time in the cold air, she ran back. I was discretely busy for a few more minutes. Then I ran home, too. Pristine was gone, and the doors were locked. I felt bad about being left outside. I didn't like being cold either. In an instant, the dark feelings of anger closed in on me. I had been forgotten.

In the new version of the same event, I made it happen the way it should have the first time. After I found the door closed, I saw O'mamma inside peeking out. I shouted at her so loud that the glass in the door rattled.

"What was the hurry?" I yelled. *"I was behind a bush. Make an effort! Call my name!"*

She rushed to open the door, saying "sorry." The next day she waited patiently, and she called my name. I was amazed. Successful assertion had brought great results that gave my step the lightness of walking on air.

With the help of that good feeling, I moved on to the most dreaded dark side feeling, aggression. I was relieved to find out O'mamma believed there was one kind of aggression that wouldn't knock you off your socially acceptable pedestal.

"Reacting forcefully to the danger of bodily harm or property theft is considered important to the duty to protect," she said. "And when the way you respond makes you a hero someday, you'll receive admiration and possibly a medal. "

I already knew that, so why hadn't I been quick to act aggressively? My response was not automatic. Why not? When I placed myself there at the scene again, I saw I was in a quandary about what to do with the messy details of what might follow decisive action.

"What if I have to deal with having a horribly hairy critter in my mouth, or worse, a piece of him? Will I end up fighting with my conscience if I bite another canine?" Those two scenarios showed the kind of thoughts interfering with swift and sure reactions.

The problem was clear. I was worrying while I was supposed to be aggressively protecting. No one can worry and protect at the same time. That's just not possible.

After having imagined so many old scenes, I had gotten rid of almost all regret about past failures involving assertion. Now, I had to prepare my spirit for decisive, aggressive action. I was ready to practice attacks and to aim a few at criminal canines.

I returned to an awful event from last summer. What happened to one poor chicken by way of the teeth of one mean pooch has plagued me ever since it happened.

The scrawny, spoiled, bad boy had crossed our perimeter at the gap in the fence separating our farm from the park. I still remembered the sounds of screams from the mother and teenage girl and the crying as they saw their dog sinking his teeth into the back of a helpless hen. I had sprung into action and run at him, but I am ashamed to say I hesitated to bite.

Now that I've been freed to aggress like I should, I pictured my first bite, the second, the retreat, and the blood. *"Look at you whimpering!"* I yelled, *"Run home to your mamma."*

Then, for good measure I flashed a row of canine cuspid at the women. They were unaware they had become the first sapiens to experience a Dark Side Smile.

Victory was sweet, even imagining victory was sweet.

I pictured myself in action. Written across the back of my red jacket were the words "A Dominant Force for the Good of All Beings" in big, black letters. It thrilled me to have a champion's title. I continued choosing rivals from past battles and creating scenes that were wildly daring.

There I was a proud canine elevated to a higher plane, walking on air with the power to assert every side I had. I reckoned I could do anything anyone else could do even write poems better than O'mamma.

"King of the Hill" was the first one I wrote...

The world is my toilet.
I piss where I will.
Unless someone stops me,
I'm King of his hill.

"Ha! Ha! Ha! Thank you, O'mamma. Arthur Dogson Todd, is having fun at his home inside himself!"

Part 3: Victory

Question: How many times did I have to relive bad memories before my suffering was healed?

Answer: A lot.

Question: How many new versions of old stories did I need to create to find my warrior self?

Answer: A lot.

For weeks I took O'mamma's advice and practiced reviewing past events. By putting in a lot of time, I got good at it. Like a classic canine thinker, I would relax on my upholstered chair with head hanging down at the Precise Angle. I pictured this, and I pictured that. The stories were filled with assertion and aggression and ended in sweet victory.

As I worked on the events, I noticed their impact on my spirit weakening. In fact, by the tenth time or so the effect had become so weak it was as boring as watching a field of deflated balloons unable to rise up on a breeze and dangle their strings.

A feeling of acceptance floated through me. Regret and shame had disappeared. *"The dark side is as lifeless as the balloons."* It was no longer a threat to my popularity.

The rude behavior that had caused me to be called "obnoxious" was gone, too. Magically, I was left peaceful, yet energetic and strong.

O'mamma said naming new feelings was an important step in hanging on to healing, so I called this one "a comfortable confidence."

Even the guy in the old King of the Hill poem had been transformed. When I looked back at what he wrote, it seemed angry, defiant, and crude, but sadly not confident. *"He sounded more like Huff and Puff in the story about the wolf,"* I thought.

I returned to the hill and wrote this.

KING OF THE HILL
(new version)

Although at dawn it was not zero,
Compared to sixty-four,
Thirty-two degrees in spring
Is cold enough to nip my nose
As I head out the door.

I drink in sundry frozen smells,
Odors if you will
Arising from the dampened ground,
Wafting o'er
From up the hill.

With jaunty attitude and speed
Up to a discreet spot, I hurry.
Beyond our fence row,
Near a tree
I cock my leg with little worry.

No one's turned up.
No protests made.
So I amble back with crown in place
And a royal countenance displayed
Enhancing my mere canine face.

Coming down off the hill and stepping along to the rhythm of the new verses, I arrived at the massive boxwood by the right of the green steps leading to our front porch.

There stood O'mamma. She opened the door with the rattley glass and smiled. "Come in, Arthur. It's cold out there."

ONE POEM, TWO AUTHORS

W as O'mamma upset about the other afternoon? Did she remember how impatient I became? What about the Howl of All Howls? Did it hurt her ears? When I lost patience, *Big-Daddy-Dawg*, I lost control.

I knew my job was to be an emotional support, but a dog can take just so much. I had my own emotions to support.

Sure. I knew excuses were considered excuses, but it hadn't been my fault entirely. That poem about Ohno and Mother Nature's cruelty drove me to it.

I worried that the crude, rude word in the first "King of the Hill" might have bad consequences.

"I know you changed your first poem. I like the new version better. It's jaunty!" She sounded enthusiastic.

My tail curled upward as worry evaporated.

"I think you and I should write something jaunty together."

Surprise! Surprise! Surprise... even when it's good, it's still a shock. I froze like the squirrels did when I used to sneak up on them. Then I ran like they did, not with a nut in my mouth... but with an idea in my mind.

"Okay, great!" I thought. With ears perked and head as high as I could manage, I wagged.

So the two authors put their words together to tell a mid-winter story. I agreed to Mother Nature being mentioned though only briefly.

IN THE JANUARY THAW
by O'mamma and Arthur D. Todd

Two hibernating creatures turned over in their
   lair.
They yawned and yawned themselves awake
With mouths as open as their tiny jaws could
   bear.
The moon sent many beams of light to dance on
   every row
Of pointy, opalescent teeth sparkling like the
   snow.
Rolling side to side, they gained strength 'til they
   could stand.
Standing led to stepping. Soon their steps
   became a stroll.
Scampering in the cold moonlight caused a hunger
   pang or two
So they pressed against the chickens' door
To try to make it let them through.

The garbage bin was next to weather their attack

Any little morsel found would be a midnight snack.

When we awoke, the smell of skunk seeped beneath the kitchen door.

That's how we knew what had arrived... the January Thaw!

Toward the end of January, Mother Nature halts her coldest spell.

She takes a break for a winter nap and kindly gives us one as well.

Sunshine and a bright blue sky bring warmth and fun for several days.

Pristine and I don't stay inside... we go out to work and play.

I'm only in a sweater, my red cable knit that's new

Pristine has on her favorite, the one that's bone and blue.

O'mamma fluffs the guarding beds, making sure they're in the sun,

In case we need to lie and rest when work and play are done.

Fast and faster toward the barn, our noses to the ground we run.

Finding odors in the mud, we investigate them one by one.

At dusk, we start to yelp and bark Warnings as the night comes near,

All predators must understand Pristine and I are guarding here.

For those we love, to whom we're bound,
At house and barn, we'll stand our ground
Even if we have to fight!
Even if we have to bite!
Canines are united!
Against creatures of the night
In the January Thaw.

PALTRY POULTRY

Part 1: Attacked

I had a fight with a chicken! Not just any chicken. I had a fight with The Cock of the Walk at Misty Meadows Farm.

Who could come away from something like that and proudly say, *"I bit a bird!"* How popular would that make me? About as popular as a bully! No one would understand my side without a long, detailed explanation. You see, he's no regular little birdie.

Sure, he looks like one covered with white and brown feathers. He's got the usual wings, two scrawny legs, along with three small decorative features, one comb and two wattles. But behind his legs, he has built-in weaponry, semi-concealed at that. Besides all that, he has a bad attitude.

O'mamma and Mr. Cliff have made sure the rest of us know it's the rooster's yard as well as ours. When more than one of us, or one kind of us, uses the same space, sapiens call it "sharing." We're supposed to share the yard, and all of us do what we naturally do when we're there.

Sharing is part of being fair, and my sapiens say being fair is what allows you to hold up your head and tail with pride.

The rooster doesn't pay attention to Mr. Cliff's message. If he does hear it, he doesn't care because he wants the yard all to himself. He and his eight wives, a total of thirty-six pounds of chicken, spread out and take up the whole place.

From the top of the fencepost, he stands guard over the hens while they work to get food. If there aren't any hawks in the sky, he joins them on the ground. They peck around in the grass for bugs, seeds, and tender shoots of plants. That's their fresh food. There's dry food, too, in the henhouse. Hens need a lot of both to make eggs.

Most birds in a flock come from the same kind of egg, but our rooster and his wives come from four different kinds. Three hens are certified black and white barred rocks. Four are silver-laced wyandottes, and one is a cute, little white leghorn.

Milling around in the middle of a bunch of females from any group hasn't ever been a problem for me. While I'm working, my focus is on the job to be done. Protection is serious business. I hardly notice who is nearby, and I certainly don't interact. That could cause a major problem.

Suddenly, one developed. As I look back, I can see I should have expected it. The cute, little leghorn was pecking closer and closer to my post in the yard. She's slender and has a sweet little comb that falls to the side, bright red and pretty.

Don't get me wrong. I have absolutely no interest in finding a girlfriend from a poultry flock. She stood out because she was the only leghorn and because O'mamma talked about how cute she was. Besides that, unlike many canine brethren, I am committed to Pristine my current and, of course, canine girlfriend.

I was carefully sniffing around in the grass for a possible intruder scent when I was taken by surprise. That "domesticated" fowl, the rooster, was running toward me.

I saw him coming, so I thought I'd have a man-to-man discussion with him. I wanted to explain that a guy cannot control a female's attraction to him and that I had no romantic feelings toward his hen.

Not ever having communicated one-on-one with anyone in the poultry group, I was momentarily frozen to the spot. He mistook my hesitation for weakness and instantly attacked. With a lot of wing action, he rushed at me flapping without saying anything.

The wind from the flapping created lift and raised him off the ground about a foot to the level of my head. All the while, he was flogging me with his claws and spurs. Those spurs were like daggers thrust so fast they looked blurry. He missed my eyes and got me near the ear.

O'mamma heard me screaming loud, high-pitched barks that said, *"Stop! You're hurting me!"* In the throes of agony, I opened and shut my mouth in a fast one-two rhythm snapping at him with sharp canine teeth. All I ended up with was a mouthful of feathers. O'mamma arrived on the scene just as he backed off.

We were in the standoff phase of the battle. He faced me with head erect and eyes unblinking. O'mamma later said that was the moment his "imperious nature was unmasked." I gave him the sideways shoulder stance and stared straight ahead making my eyes appear as beady as possible.

O'mamma told Mr. Cliff later that my tail was between my legs. She said it ran up along my midsection protecting what few bits of maleness I have left. With ears flattened against my head and shoulders hunched tightly up against my neck, I was ready to spring myself forward into action or backward into retreat.

O'mamma grabbed the green lunge whip she carries in the yard just because of him and his combative nature. I began to slink away worrying if biting a chicken of our own flock might be an unforgivable offense like biting a family member. Where was that family line drawn? I didn't know how to measure to tell.

It looked obvious that she held the rooster responsible for the fight. She chased him with the whip until that thin, green string part of it wrapped around his feet. Then she dragged the hobbled bird far away from where he had attacked me. He didn't give in to his loser status. Instead, he wriggled free of the string and stared at her from a sideways position ready to fly up and attack again.

In an effort to dominate him, she whacked the string on the ground so fast it whistled as it went down. Because of her accuracy with that thing, O'mamma was able to graze his wing.

The rooster stood there so still and poised that he looked exactly like the porcelain rooster statue we have on top of the bookcase near the kitchen.

Everyone in the yard stayed still and quiet. Their eyes followed as she turned her back on him and walked slowly away with the string of the whip trailing behind her. She was fast enough to turn and whack the rooster if he followed her. He knew it, so for today the fight was over.

I had to accept that the rooster had more on his mind than danger from outside threats. Anyone and everyone not in his flock was a dangerous intruder. He acted out of jealousy and got aggressive at the sight of any of us near his hens.

I'd been mistaken when I used to assume the rooster and I had been working side by side under Mr. Cliff, our Top Guard.

All I could do was remind myself of the need for new rules about crossing the yard when I was alone. The reality of the circumstances was critical for making sound decisions. I made a list of the following facts because they are real and impossible to deny.

1. I am an attractive male. Females of all species will notice me. Some may approach.

2. A guy with eight wives cannot possibly pay enough attention to each one. So being unattended to and possibly lonely, one or more of his hens may approach. That is a risk to my safety.

3. The cute little Leghorn is in a marriage arranged by O'mamma. Females who are trapped in undesirable circumstances will look for someone to provide a way out for them. She may approach. This fact makes her an extra high risk.

I decided to avoid the whole paltry poultry situation by being constantly aware of everyone's location in the yard. No more meandering around gathering my thoughts would be allowed. I looked at The Flock differently. O'mamma did too. She said it was like a cult with a control-crazed leader. Going through their space had to be approached like I was going through dangerous enemy territory.

The danger was real, but the challenge excited me!

As far as the rooster's personal growth went, I doubted that O'mamma and I had been able to communicate anything to him. If one of his wives got attention from another guy, would he do the same thing again?

Of course! He wasn't the type to look back and question his own behavior. So we had to accept that he didn't learn a thing from our run-in today.

Since it was always going to be his yard too, we decided to work around his fowl nature. I hoped Misty Meadows would be big enough for both of us.

Part 2: The Rooster Reigns

A s the days went by, I had to admit to myself that I couldn't stand my ground against the rooster. He was everywhere I was flapping his wings for added speed as he chased me across the yard. Like a duck landing legs first on a pond, he tried to land on me with both weapons poised to strike my face.

Spurs, his weapons are called spurs. They're on the back of his legs, hidden from view when you meet him head-on. In a blink, he can turn his ugly chicken feet up toward the sky and fly down with them pointed at his target, me.

He kept up with my exact location. I could feel him watching every step I took. Instead of being the one to scan the yard for predators like I used to, the in-house predator was scanning my yard for me. Now all the ground from the house to the barn belonged to him. It wasn't my territory anymore. *Sigh...*

How could I observe, evaluate, and perform while I was being stalked? My superior ability to concentrate had been stolen. My proven guarding routine had stopped in the last set of my old tracks. The new tracks didn't go anywhere. The only place for me to go was into the house or barn. The barn door was left open all day, so I chose the house.

Since birds were awake from dawn until dusk, I became homebound. Instead of finding the most comfortable spot in the sun or shade for guarding, I lay huddled in a pile of blankets on the family bed. Guarding our whole place from the second floor was difficult.

I was able to manage some successful strikes by running down the front stairs as soon as there was the slightest noise indicating an intruder. All the running down and out the door and then back up was very tiring.

I began napping more. That's one reason why I missed the fox-on-chicken and hawk-on-hen excitement.

Fortunately for the rooster's wives, O'mamma covered the fox incident with her broom and screams, and the farrier's boys fought off the hawk.

The rooster was making a big mistake by rivaling me. Why couldn't he understand that his jealousy made him act crazy?

For the best protection of the yard, we needed to have constant monitoring. The fact was his wives were vulnerable without both of us. Two guards could cover more ground than one.

Mr. Cliff and O'mamma were taking way too long to see the changes in me. My behavior and my posture told a story of misery. Without much exercise, my pace became slower and weaker. My spirit was sinking.

Why weren't a mental health worker and a property manager quicker to notice? I began to feel taken for granted. I tried not to be bitter, but that was only a part of the reason for my deteriorating mood. I began remembering things from the past that made me angry.

When I was a pup, I'd noticed most sapiens liked to watch each other and write about what they saw on their screens. They took photos of faces almost every day. That took time away from what they were supposed to do, keep their eyes on us and stay on top of how healthy we were.

There was a law that said those who deserved and needed their guardians' care were the young, the old, indoor pets, and the rest of the animals they kept. If they didn't take proper care of us, they'd have to go to jail and that was not fun. It was a time-out room where there was nothing to do but eat and sleep. And the only screen they'd be allowed to watch was on a television.

One time I saw a man on TV say, "If you see changes in the behavior of anyone you love like if they look sad, if they don't come out of the bedroom, and if they stop communicating, you should buy them this medicine I'm selling and tell them to take twelve steps."

He asked things like how do you know... if your kids are on drugs... if your husband has tired blood... if your parents have Old Timer's? His answer to every question was, "Their Behavior Changes!"

My behavior had changed. *"Please sapiens, Hurry up and notice before it's too late."*

I already looked sad. I stayed in the bedroom all day. The only other sign I could give was to stop communicating. For two entire days and nights, I did not bark, growl, or howl.

Howling was the hardest of all to keep to myself. I loved to howl when she sang. It was a special sort of togetherness.

That was what got O'mamma's attention—no howling. I knew she missed it when I heard her say, "I feel out of touch with Arthur. I think something's wrong."

Usually, that's when Mr. Cliff gives the "you worry too much" speech. He didn't. Instead, he said, "He looks sad, and he's always in bed before I am. I think that rooster is getting the best of him."

"*Way to go, Mr. C., you know how a guy looks when he feels defeated.*" Help had arrived.

Finally, my misery was being seen for what it was. They both understood that the entire rhythm of my life had been changed by an enemy we all thought was a friend. Sapiens say that's the worst kind of disappointment.

They talked about solutions like rooster relocation, confinement for life, and armed guards. One of their strongest beliefs has always been that everyone deserved a forever home. It used to make us feel secure, but now it meant that relocation was out of the question.

The rooster hated us for trying to control how unfair he was. Confining him for life would have ruined the lives of everyone else here. That bird would've squawked and crowed until we all went crazy.

He was the only bully we knew, but I found out he wasn't the only one in the world. A group called the Society for Complainers with No Particular Cause (SC-No-PC) was founded by bullies. They were under pressure from the authorities to stop hurting others and to become kind-hearted and fair-minded. Being insulted by that demand made them so mad they retaliated by becoming the loudest of all protestors.

I wanted to get the rooster signed up as a member so he could take his attitude to their rallies. Then he'd come home tired and leave us alone! I would have even been willing to run his campaign to be elected president. That way, he could have moved into the White Coop, the headquarters of the SC-No-PC. Wouldn't that have been a win-win situation!

Mr. Cliff and O'mamma agreed that provoking him would be a mistake, so they decided on armed guards.

"Arthur must have a guard because he deserves to be happy at work! Nothing should get in the way of his concentration. We depend on him."

Great choice! My job to protect our place had been declared valuable, and I had been, too. I walked with ears perked and tail curled. O'mamma needed to have a "Tails Up" mantra ready for times like this.

Unfortunately, it seemed like every promising solution ended up having something not quite right getting in the way of full-on happiness. I couldn't stop thinking how strange things had become. Misty Meadows now had two sapiens protecting the farm's only canine guard from a chicken. Had this ever happened on any other farm? I doubted that.

Also, what they considered "armed" was odd and a little disappointing because of the weaponry. O'mamma carried a six-foot-long bamboo branch from our cane break. All that Mr. Cliff had for battle was his metal cane, the blue folding one with the black rubber tip.

One of them walked on my right side every time I crossed the yard to the new barn and pasture. Some days, I had to stand near our horses' legs and wait for a guard to walk me back home for supper.

For about a week, I felt great. The protection and their company kept my tail up and my step lively. Soon, I realized that this was not a good life because I didn't have real freedom. What I longed for was lying at a guarding post anywhere I chose. *"That would be real freedom,"* I said. "It's what I lost."

I decided it was ridiculous as well as wrong for one bad guy to have the power to make life bad for all of the hard-working, good citizens at Misty Meadows. If the criminal were under control, life would be good again. I needed to find a way to solve the problem permanently.

One evening after supper, we were in our usual places in the living room. Pristine was on the chair next to O'mamma. Mr. Cliff was in his man chair with the remote, and I was stretched out on the couch on my fake sheepskin.

A show was on TV about a court where sapiens go to complain about other sapiens. Joking around with Mr. Cliff, O'mamma laughed when she said, "Arthur should take the rooster to Judge Robin."

Why not? It would be the best place to complain because it's a judge's job to help with anything that wasn't fair in your life. I'd seen her fix equine and canine problems, and a bird problem once in a while. When she talked about her own canines, the love made her eyes dance.

O'mamma said she saw some charming bad guys win the judge to their side. I couldn't believe she would find my bad guy attractive when she saw those scrawny legs and concealed weapons.

Judge Robin Flockker lives in Manhattan with her husband, Avian. All of her children and grandchildren live nearby. Most sapiens in America know about her just like they know about Mother Nature and other famous women. But, Mother Nature and Judge Robin are the most powerful of all. If they say so, that's what happens. That's what had better happen.

I didn't know how to get in touch with Mother Nature. I had only one chance, and that would be with Judge Robin.

Upstairs at a ComfLev1 station, I thought about what I would say and what she would say. I practiced my statements a few times. Then I practiced my part and listened for her part.

Part 3: 13th Circuit Court

OFFICIAL TRANSCRIPT

OF

COURT PROCEEDINGS

13th Circuit Court

JUDGE ROBIN FLOCKKER PRESIDING

A. Falcon, Court Officer

Plaintiff: Arthur D. Todd

Defendant: Rooster *aka* Cock of the Walk at Misty Meadows Farm

PROCEEDINGS

A. FALCON: All rise. The 13th Circuit Court is now in session, Judge Robin Flockker presiding.

JUDGE: I see we have a dog as plaintiff and a very handsome bird as defendant today.

Falcon, please make sure our litigants are comfortable on the stools behind their respective tables.

Plaintiff and Defendant are seated at tables on stools sufficiently high to allow for their heads and chests to be visible to Her Honor.

My understanding is that the plaintiff is seeking an injunction against the defendant, something about taking up too much room in the yard. Sounds petty, but I'll hear it, anyway.

Mr. Dog, oh, how special... You have a last name other than your species. Mr. Todd, state your complaint to the Court, please.

MR. TODD: Your Honor, I have been a resident and hard worker at Misty Meadows Farm for ten years, five years longer than the Rooster. My status is adoptee. I have the paperwork. My birth date is January eighth. I was adopted on April eighteenth. I was chosen because of my abili...

JUDGE: Not important. Not important. Present relevant information only, Mr. Todd.

MR. TODD: The defendant arrived in the spring of the year two thousand and seven as a homeless chick with no papers. Over a period of five years, he has expanded his territory from the enclosed area of his coop at the edge of the yard to the entire yard. He has instructed his flock of hens to occupy every inch of space that was originally shared by all species... canines, equines, felines, and fowl, as well as the undomesticated. He is combative with anyone who crosses or occupies territory that should be shared.

My case is based on the fact that he has no claim to the sole use of territory other than that which was originally given him, the eight-foot by ten-foot area in front of his coop door which is clearly marked because it's fenced with chicken wire. That area of eighty square feet plus the area inside the coop of thirty square feet exceeds the required amount allowed for chicken health and welfare.

JUDGE: No larger than a prison cell, Mr. Todd. Does he have a back door?

MR. TODD: His back door goes...

JUDGE: It's a yes or no answer to my question, Mr. Todd. Yes or no. He does. He doesn't. Pick one.

MR. TODD: No, his back door goes into the barn, not a yard. He has the inside of the barn.

JUDGE: Okay. He has the barn, the whole barn?

MR. TODD: No, only the right side.

JUDGE: Very good. See, it's simple. Yes or no, and then you explain.

MR. TODD: Yes, Your Honor, and he's mean to others, even his wives. He has an aggressive character.

JUDGE: Don't care, Mr. Todd, unless, of course, you are his wife or you are claiming assault.

MR. TODD: Yes, I mean no, Your Honor. I'm not his wife, but, yes, he has assaulted me, and that's part of my complaint. He causes me such fear that I can't do my best work when I'm on my guarding bed at a ComfLev2 station outdoors. If I get up to chase a squirrel, I have to look over my shoulder so often that I can't concentrate. My performance is down.

I must always run fast across the yard to the barn because he chases me with his weapons ready to strike. In fact, he carries and conceals spurs, which are weapons, without a permit. That's against the law, isn't it?

JUDGE: I ask the questions, Mr. Todd. This is my playhouse, my show, my rules, Mr. Todd. Is that clear?

MR. TODD: Yes, Your Honor, but I do have a written account describing the first of several serious assaults. That's when I thought one of his eight wives liked me and he was jealous, so he attacked me.

JUDGE: Don't care. Don't care. You can't know what he felt. Guessing is not a basis for fact. But, I'm curious. I'll take a look at it, anyway. Falcon, please bring me the paperwork.

Several minutes pass as Your Honor reads.

All I see here is a minor kerfuffle, some chasing and hollering. Maybe he was playing with you. Boys like to play. I know. I have grandsons. No blood is reported here.

MR. TODD: Your Honor, he's carrying weapons with no permit. He pierced my skin with them, but I didn't bleed. Puncture wounds don't bleed, but they can count as an injury even if they don't show up in photos.

JUDGE: Did I ask a question? You don't speak if I didn't ask a question. I'm reading. The title of this is "Paltry Poultry." Mr. Todd, those are not nice words for such beautiful birds. Who wrote this?

Plaintiff lowered his head; his chin is against his chest. Speech is muffled by posture.

MR. TODD: O'mamma.

JUDGE: Yo Mamma! My Mamma?

MR. TODD: Oh, no, Your Honor. My Mamma. We call her O'mamma. It's the name of an Italian snack cake. It's sweet, and so is she.

JUDGE: Time to review your case, Mr. Todd.

You bring a complaint that a twenty-two-pound dog, no special breed, is being threatened and supposedly in danger of continuing harm by the actions of a four-pound bird with alleged concealed weapons. Said dog cannot perform his guarding duties. As you, yourself stated, you are unable to get your duff up off the comfy guarding bed to work because this alleged brute of a bird is looking at you.

Moreover, the dog and one of the bird's wives want to flirt without the husband caring or expressing his concern. Impossible!

Additionally, and incredibly, the dog was raised by a woman named for a Twinkie baked in Italy. Or maybe half-baked!

Whereupon, Her Honor tilted her head and smiled coyly at the spectators.

Does this review of the facts of your proof sound ridiculous to you, Mr. Todd? Does it make sense? If it doesn't make sense, it's not true, you know.

MR. TODD: I think it makes sense, Your Honor. If I can explain further...

JUDGE: No! I am speaking.

Now, I have never lived on a farm. No farms left in Manhattan. They were developed a long time ago. My children and grandchildren never lived on a farm either. We have, however, seen a lot of birds. They are all over our city... in the trees, on the fountains and sidewalks, at the park, on the rooftops, and so on. Even so, I have never seen a bird with concealed weapons harass a dog in New York City.

It is ridiculous to ask me to accept as true that a farm animal is carrying concealed weapons with him, not allowing anyone to step in "his" yard by way of threat of harm to them.

By the way, Mr. Todd, are you aware of how tall the defendant is?

MR. TODD: Fifteen inches, Your Honor.

JUDGE: *Whereupon, Her Honor threw her head back and cackled.*

Fifteen inches! You're a fool. If it doesn't make sense, it's not true, Mr. Todd. Your case makes the least sense of any I have heard in this Court.

This is my ruling. The plaintiff has been given sufficient time and opportunity in order for him to show proof in a case of a paltry nature, to use your own word, Mr. Todd. I find no proof to support your claim. Therefore, your case against the Rooster is dismissed with prejudice.

Whereupon, A. Falcon, Court Officer, escorted both parties from the courtroom and reunited them with their common guardian O'mamma who had been waiting in the hallway.

ONE BUSY DAY

Part 1: Morning

Guys are impatient when we're hungry. Of all of us at Misty Meadows, Zip was the most impatient, just a hair ahead of Cody who was a nose ahead of me. Often he demanded to be fed by rudely pawing and kicking his stall door.

Bang! Bang! Bang! Cody copied him, and Zip stopped. Strange how that happened! It made me wonder if Cody might be working for Zip by delivering his messages like Secretariats do. *"Somehow that didn't come out right, but you know what I mean."*

I'd like to add here that even though Mr. Cliff and I are guys, we've never caused any kind of trouble over food. We do admit to having followed with our eyes giving O'mamma the Dying from Hunger Look (DFHL), but we've never growled or stamped our feet, nothing that extreme.

To be ready for anything, including three demanding horses, O'mamma usually mixes up one week's worth of their meals in advance. The Girl Scout motto "Be Prepared" that she learned a long time ago has helped her with a lot of things. When she got enough done ahead of time, she looked forward to a happy start to every day.

What's called "food" for a horse isn't what Mr. Cliff or I would want to eat. Alfalfa, rice bran, beet pulp, and flax meal are what they get. I bet it tastes as good as grass to their taste buds, maybe even better.

O'mamma dips into the forty and fifty-pound bags for a cup or two of each ingredient and adds herbs and carrots before putting it all in zip-lock bags. At feeding time, she pours the mixture into buckets quickly so she can prevent rude behavior.

I don't know the exact amounts, but I do know they get more cups in cold weather and fewer in spring and summer. It's about the calorie thing that makes me feel sorry for myself. She calls it "calorie mindfulness." I call it *"calorie cruelty."* Mr. Cliff says he "disbelieves" it.

I have to admit that her ideas about healthy eating keep us all in good shape, but we're supposed to accept it's because of something that can't be seen but still can be counted. Without some kind of proof, I'm not a believer in anything I can't see or smell especially if it makes me unhappy.

It sounded similar to that thing about how many angels could dance on the head of a pin. Sapiens wasted a lot of energy debating that one. No one could see angels on a pin, and no one can see calories. Same idea...

Sapiens are the only warm-blooded beings I know who have been silly enough to fight for illogical ideas as if they were true. Even though some of them believed fighting and arguing were a waste of time, the know-it-alls acted like it was worth the unhappiness they caused and the friends they lost.

I got the angel part from Mr. Cliff. He brought that up last Sunday when he was told his cake and ice cream were filled with "empty calories." He shouted that he could not and would not believe calories were in his cake and they were empty.

"There are as many empty calories in my cake as there are angels dancing on the head of a pin." Now he hates the calorie thing as much as I do.

"Filled with empty..." Whoa, horsey! Somebody is good at making up stories filled with empty words.

Part 2: Late Morning

While Cody and Lace were grazing in the field, O'mamma finished filling the food bags for the week. "Time to eat," she shouted. Then she whistled for them to come in. They ignored her.

Whistle. Ignore. Whistle. Ignore. Finally, out of patience with them, she ran outside and jumped into the orange Kubota Four Wheel Drive that she calls "Diesel Boy." (DB)

O'mamma ran DB at full speed, chasing the horses across the fields. They ran galloping and turning one way and then another going farther and farther up the hill. Just like she was on another horse, she circled around and herded them toward the barn.

Pristine and I watched from a safe distance as they came running into the fenced dry lot. We ran after them barking.

As O'mamma latched the gate, I heard her singing a cowgirl song she made up about herself and the horses. She sings it when no one else is around. I might be the only one who knows, but she's never told me not to tell. The song goes like this:

> *You can run all you want.*
> *You can love how it feels.*
> *You may have four feet,*
> *But I have four wheels.*
> *Kubota cowgirls run with their wheels!*

She laughed out loud. "Ha! Ha! Ha!" I could tell O'mamma felt great, kind of like me when I've chased every squirrel out of our yard. I say *"Ha! Ha! Ha!"* and a few other things.

The orange Kubota FWD stayed parked at the barn ready for other work like moving feed and sawdust or checking on the fences and fallen trees.

We walked to the house to eat lunch.

Part 3: Afternoon

O'mamma spent most of the afternoon in the drippy rain washing her car. Earlier in the week, she had tried to have it professionally polished. When she called the car dealer where she bought it sixteen years ago, the service department manager said they would do a thorough wash and buff for nineteen ninety-five.

She happily drove to their huge garage and pulled in. After inspecting the car closely, her service advisor said in a solemn voice that he saw a serious problem, tree sap on the roof and trunk.

To promise to get her car clean was not possible, he said, even with their best one hundred ninety-nine dollar, full-service job.

Then, he inhaled deeply which puffed out his chest and tilted his chin upward slightly making it necessary for him to look down his nose to see O'mamma as he spoke. "Most of the cars we service are kept in their owners' garages," he explained, "so tree sap is not something we have to deal with."

Fortunately, O'mamma had grown up with three women who were especially creative cleaners. What she had learned from them gave her the confidence to speed away from all the progress that's been made in modern car care and go back forty years to her antiquated family ways. With a little effort and good old-fashioned Octagon yellow soap, she vowed to clean the car herself until it looked like new.

She knew that a big garage wasn't the best place for washing cars, anyway. Outside in the rain worked better for getting off stubborn dirt because her "friend" Mother Nature helped out with a long pre-soak and rinse.

Mother Nature's help came through. The yellow soap dissolved the sap. "The old ways still work!" she said. "I love success!" Her car sparkled, and she still had her nineteen ninety-five.

I didn't hear another victorious "Ha! Ha! Ha!" She must have been celebrating inside herself because by then she was too tired to shout about anything.

Part 4: Evening

F inally finished with the car, O'mamma fixed a cup of tea before she started supper. At 4:30, the sky was already getting dark. "Time to close up the chickens for the night and feed the horses and cats again," she said. Fatigue began setting in for all of us as we trudged onward toward the barn.

In the last stall for the last of the chores, O'mamma pulled down a bale of hay from the tall pile. After she cut the twine holding it together, she picked up three flakes, one each for Zip, Cody, and Lace. She sensed someone looking down at her from above.

Yup, Pup, there on the wall between the stalls sat a new cat, a stranger, not one of us. No matter what I called him, the point was he was exactly not the kind of company we should welcome at any hour or at any door. And the truth was he wasn't really "new." Pristine and I had chased him the day before. O'mamma didn't see the battle we had with him, so he was new to her.

On our early morning patrol along the park perimeter, we met Intruder Cat for the first time. He was sitting motionless on a fencepost in the covered arena across from the barn. I profiled him immediately as someone with No-Friends-for-Good-Reasons. We had gotten close enough to feel the chilling effects of his aggressive scowl.

The scars above his eyes were probably from fights with other cats. I said to Pristine, *"Careful! That's a dangerous, battled-scarred bully."*

Cautiously, we moved slowly toward him. Suddenly, he crouched like he was about to spring onto our backs. He couldn't. There were two of us and only one of him. Realizing that, he changed his strategy and began swiping with alternating paws from his higher position on the post.

What a scene! He whirled around with us circling below him in the sand. We were jumping up and barking while he hunched down as low as he could going toward our eyes with his claws.

For safety, I decided to change strategies. We turned our backs on him and calmly strutted away, tails up. We didn't bother to check to see if he was coming after us, didn't need to because a bully-coward wouldn't dare to follow, anyway. Like I said, I had him profiled.

After that skirmish, I detected his scent around the girls' room in the barn. That's the cats' room. I never actually saw him in there, but phew he was strong. I presumed he still had possession of all his parts even though he didn't act like it.

Tired but still true to herself at the moment, O'mamma looked up and said in an unusually sharp tone, "Who are you? I'll give you some food, but we don't share litter pans."

Drawing the line at the litter pans said a lot about his unwelcome status. I knew for sure the ruffian wasn't civilized enough to have agreed to use a litter pan, anyway. He probably didn't even know what one looked like.

But why did she offer him food? I understood at the moment that was all she could manage to say as tired as she was and as polite as she likes to be.

I think I'm right when I say, *"Understanding is the best thing you can give someone who's dog-tired."*

THE HONEY TOAST PROMISE

Part 1: A Sweet Routine

All of a sudden, I noticed O'mamma doing certain things at the same time each day. She called them "routines." I agreed with the ones that were sensible like turning on the house alarm at 10 p.m. every night to let it listen for intruders while we slept. So was pressing the numbers on the box in the morning to turn it off.

"Routines make life easier because we choose once and for all what time we do each thing," she said. "Our minds won't get tired if we don't use them to decide everything all over again every day."

But others made absolutely no sense like feeding the cats before me and Pristine. That decision was based on a myth that says cats will meow themselves to death if they don't eat first. O'mamma said she might as well save time and feed the horses second because we were already at the barn.

"Really!" What about my time waiting for food? Every minute counted when I was hungry. *"Routines are routinely getting in my way!"*

"They have a purpose for the good of all, Arthur," she said. "One day you'll understand."

Then, a new, delicious routine made the question of who ate first less important. It began with O'mamma's love for honey. She used to sing about it to the tune of "Happy Birthday." "I love honey, do you?" were the first words to her song.

While the word "honey" slowly flowed out with her breath, Pristine and I relaxed and breathed out, too. A special feeling floated over us like a happy cloud. We'd move near to her so we could enjoy it close together.

Our honey-loving mamma must have remembered those sweet times when she invented the new morning routine, the Honey Toast Sharing Ceremony (HTSC). It was so wonderful, special, and perfect. Nothing else we did had ever reached such a high level of taste and togetherness.

To see it, you should come by at 7:30, stand in the mudroom and peek through the window. We're there by the chair at the kitchen table ready for O'mamma to begin.

I'm on the side by the hand she eats with. Pristine is on the other. O'mamma carries her tea and a plate with honey toast to the table and sits down between us.

First, we thank the bees. After that, there's no more talking.

With a deep breath and a sip of tea, O'mamma starts the Ceremony. Then she begins on the first half of the honey toast. Staring straight ahead into space, she slowly takes small bites. It seems like forever until the sharing begins, but it always does.

In the tiny moment before she offers us our first share, her breath and posture change. We can tell that her spirit is leaving the pleasure of buttery sweetness and is coming back to be with us.

I've noticed that about squirrels too. I watched one in the yard sitting near a tree motionless except for his jaws moving while he ate. He stared straight ahead. Then, there was a wide-eyed "freeze" as if he woke up from a trance. He sensed me there right before he ran.

O'mamma does the same thing right before sharing. Sitting as still as I can next to her, I stare and stop breathing. I'm copying her posture so she'll sense me there. Sapiens call it "presence." They can feel it just like the squirrels could when I synchronized with them.

O'mamma pauses as she feels my presence. She's aware again. Our eyes meet. After taking a small bite for herself, she reaches down toward us both at the same time. Each hand is offering a morsel, my share on the right and Pristine's on the left. Then, there is a quiet moment of joy as we all taste the same sweet honey and butter on toast. The day has begun with us united in pleasure and equality.

For more than a year, we enjoyed the Honey Toast Sharing Ceremony. It was repeated exactly the same way every day.

Then one afternoon, I saw O'mamma hurrying to the shed. She returned with a suitcase, took it to the bedroom, and filled it with her clothes and things from the bathroom cabinet. Before I could understand what was happening, she had already said "see you later," kissed us all goodbye, and driven off in the truck. We were upset.

Mr. Cliff was the only sapiens we had with us at home. A late sleeper, he had never seen us at the Ceremony. So not knowing anything about the sweetness of our early morning routine, he couldn't understand why we would miss it.

I moped around going from guarding post to guarding post all day long. While I was lying on the beds, my eyes opened... closed... opened... closed. Nonetheless, I kept my ears open, listening like I always do for danger.

If I'm suffering, I do it silently. That's not Pristine's style. How does she look when she's upset? Well, first she runs in circles and throws her toys in the air until she gets tired. Then, she falls into a deep sleep. I guess that's her way to escape unhappiness.

"Why is not having Honey Toast so irritating?" I asked myself. I stayed awake and spent a lot of time searching for the answer. I was unhappy.

On day three, the pattern of what was going on became clear. If you do the same thing over and over again for someone else, you become responsible for their expectation that you'll keep doing it. So, if you fill my bowl with food every day for a long time, then I'll have the right to expect food every day. If you stop, you'll cause a disturbance, maybe a ruckus, even a rebellion or a revolution. It probably would depend on how many of us you disappointed.

By the end of day three, I was convinced of it. Creating a routine was equal to making a promise. O'mamma had given us food, water, and our HTS Ceremony every day. When she stopped, that broke her promise. I was irritated. No, I was more upset than that, but it was too soon for an uprising. She wasn't back yet.

I knew what I decided was true because it made sense. I learned that a while ago in Judge Robin Flockker's court. She told me, "If it doesn't make sense, it's not true, Mr. Todd." I lost my case against the rooster because she couldn't find the sense in my story.

According to Her Honor, if it did make sense, basically, it was true. Judge Robin, the most trusted woman in America had basically said so.

O'mamma needed to be informed that breaking her promise caused unhappiness for us and disappointment that she had gone back on her promise. One time, I overheard Mr. Cliff say the truth hurts. I didn't want to hurt her, but I had to let her know. If she didn't know, she couldn't do better next time.

"If I can get the courage to speak up, I'll have a better attitude and be able to forgive her when she apologizes," I told myself.

The first time I said it softly. *"You made a routine out of the Honey Toast Sharing Ceremony. We learned to expect it. Leaving us without what you started broke your promise."*

When she returns, I'm prepared to deliver the facts of the situation.

Part 2: A Question of Trust

Seven mornings after she left with her suitcase, O'mamma was on the way home. Mr. Cliff told us to expect her any minute. Pristine and I went outside to wait on the front porch.

I wasn't feeling as bad as I did while she was gone. *"Why?"* I asked myself. She hadn't even arrived yet.

For all those days while O'mamma was away, I had kept an anti-O'mamma attitude going on. A lot of negativity and suspicion ran around in my mind. The moment we would see her again came closer, and my unhappiness about the broken promise was going away. It was a relief.

Still, I vowed to stick to my decision to follow the plan I had made. Happy or not, I would observe O'mamma's behavior with maximum attention to the details. If there were any changes in our routines without explanation, protests would be made. Negotiations would follow.

My thoughts were interrupted by the sound of her truck coming along the gravel drive. She smiled as she pulled in and waved to us. We wagged happily and ran up to her as she got out with her suitcase.

O'mamma wasted no time talking about where she'd been. She picked up right where we had left off by preparing for our morning Sharing Ceremony. Pristine and I took our places near her chair and waited.

I was feeling sentimental as my mind drifted back to the day we first learned about where honey came from. It was the day before we ever ate it with butter on toast.

O'mamma drove the truck toward the Alabama-Tennessee border to buy our first gallon. She told us insects who make honey are called bees and explained that a queen and her boyfriends and workers live in a house called a hive. There are lots of hives and thousands of bees living on one honey farm.

I was impressed and also grateful I had ended up on a farm living with only chickens, horses, and cats. An occasional bee flies by, but he goes on his way after he smells the flowers. If more than one appears, I take cover afraid of an attack.

After we parked at the honey farm, Pristine and I stayed in the truck and waited while O'mamma went up the steps to the front door. When the Bee People came out, she told them we were there to buy three gallons. The Bee Woman and her daughter happily brought the jugs all the way to our truck. O'mamma paid them, and we drove toward home.

While we were on our way back, she said we would be eating honey on toast for our health each morning. Three gallons of honey at one spoon a day, hmm... I thought we had enough for life. Recently, I overheard her say there's only one gallon left. "Hello, Bee People, we'll be back this fall."

I came out of my memory bank abruptly when I saw O'mamma already at the table with a cup of tea and the honey toast cut in half. Being in a rush for the taste of it again, we forgot to thank the bees.

As usual, O'mamma ate the first half. It was the calorie mindfulness thing again. Because she's five times bigger than us she gets more toast than we do. Then, for all three of us, she broke off morsels from the second half. We ate them slowly, piece by piece.

I noticed that the honey tasted extra, extra good. Even though *extra good* should be a good thing, I paid careful attention in case something was different. I had promised myself that I would notice every detail, so I did.

While her hand was extended holding a morsel toward my mouth, I drew back just a bit. My eyes crossed when I saw it! Home for only an hour and there was an unexplained change in the Ceremony.

Upside down! She was giving us our ceremonial morsels with the wrong side up and the right side down. Even with my eyes crossed, I could see the slight turn of her hand that caused the toast to flip. Honey and butter landed first. The change seemed to have made their flavors incredibly delicious.

A troubling conflict between suspicion and delight gave me a floating feeling and a vision of being outside myself wearing a white coat, staring at my own outstretched tongue.

Confused, I asked myself, *"Was it only because of the surge of pleasure after seven long days of deprivation, or was it something a lot more serious?"* I had didn't have time to answer my own question because O'mamma interrupted. Before she said "all gone," she spoke, another change in the Ceremony.

She told us how much she missed sharing honey toast while she was away. At night, it was worse than during the day, she said. Lying in bed alone in the dark, she pretended she was with us at the kitchen table. It was so comforting it helped her fall asleep.

An idea that could make our HTSC more delicious arose from her nighttime reverie. If the honey landed on the best place in our mouths for tasting, the Taste Bud Tongue Spot (TBTS), she knew we would enjoy the flavor even more.

O'mamma explained that taste buds helped us enjoy our food and that they were part of our tongues. Naturally, placing food directly on the TBT Spot would make the taste stronger. Right side up the toast was in the way, so why not try it upside down?

While she was explaining the reasons for the change, it made sense. But, with all the suspicion surging through my brain, I could hardly examine the logic as thoroughly and extensively as I usually did. I felt rushed into trusting. I was not ready.

Many times sapiens have promised that their plans for change would make things better even though they were already great. Often, it turned out they were just bossy know-it-alls in love with their own grand ideas trying to impose their love for themselves on the rest of us. Even if the results made the situation worse, even if we all suffered, they continued to insist on calling their way "progressive."

Whenever I heard of new ideas and plans I had never been a bit curious about, my head felt heavy and hard to hold up even though it rested on very strong shoulders.

As usual, fatigue and anger inside me made it easier to be rude even to the ones I loved. Fortunately, most of my harsh words remained unspoken thoughts like these...

"Listen, Your Bossyness, I love everything here just like it is. So does Pristine. We don't want you to fix something Pristine and I already enjoy. You could ruin it. Don't go there!"

Pristine's reactions have always been different from mine. She'd go along with any changes if they didn't sound scary. Then, if there was any doubt in her mind, she'd ignore it and agree, anyway. Then she relieved the stress of repressing uncertainty by throwing her toys around until she got tired. I would love to do that, too, and take a nap afterward.

What was there to enjoy about getting stuck with suspicion and fear about what might happen? A racing mind wasn't helpful. It wore me out when it was in high gear. I couldn't stop making triple sure that changes would be good, fair, sensible, and efficient. I envied Pristine more than ever.

I had only two choices: I could trust that O'mamma had a great idea and our happiness was safe, or I could think about every possible way it might go wrong.

The first one went against getting the comfort that suspicion can provide. The second had the power to throw me into high gear forever.

Because it was food that had passed the taste test and because I had to keep my focus on job-related things, I went with trust as my choice. I decided I would even say, *"Thank you for caring and trying and loving..."* and all the rest that went along with polite submission to ideas that weren't mine.

If I ever wanted to be worry-free and therefore happy, I told myself I had to repeat these two promises every day.

1. I will try to become more like Pristine by going along with plans I didn't make.

2. I will never give up checking the logic in thinking if it doesn't come from my own brain.

"Please let this be the final change to our beloved Honey Toast Sharing Ceremony. It can't get any better than it already is." Sigh...

BEAT THE RAT

Part 1: The Problem Explained

It all began after X-Terminator, also known as Snake, left our place. He had been at Misty Meadows all summer and fall last year. That big boy feasted on lots of rats, and eggs too. Life was good for him then.

By winter, he had eaten so many rats that most of the ones who survived got scared and ran off. Those who stayed were afraid to have more babies. At the same time that was happening, the hens took their winter break and stopped laying eggs.

O'mamma had measured X-Terminator. Well, not directly. She had seen him stretched out in front of the row of chicken nests in the old barn. By using a tape measure along the row, she could tell that he was 6' 5," six feet long and five inches around.

As big as he was, he needed a lot of food to keep him going. No eggs and not enough rats for his appetite put him in a hungry situation. Fearful of starving to death as well as never having achieved my approval to live here convinced him to move on.

How weak-willed! Someone who scared more than half of the men in the world was afraid of a little hunger? Me, I got just a cup of food a day plus treats. Even if I were starving, I wouldn't be so filled with fear I'd move out of a good home.

Snake proved that he was not as tough as me, yet half of the men in the world wouldn't be afraid if I showed up in their barns. It must be in the eyes. I'm going to practice that no-blink stare.

At first, we could only assume he was gone, but later we were sure when more rats moved in. Without the snake and with the rooster dead, the new rats didn't have any enemies. This group knew nothing about fear. They casually ate our eggs and the chickens' Laying Formula, too.

Within the very next minute after the hen had left the nest, a rat would be there eating the new egg. We all prefer our food warm, but that's ridiculous.

When O'mamma found out, she said, "We work hard to raise hens so we can have eggs." I hadn't seen her so mad since the rooster attacked me.

Before I go on with the rest of the story, I need to tell about the hard work we do to bring new chickens into our family.

There's no rooster to father babies anymore thanks to one hunger-crazed possum, so we have to adopt. Two-day-old chicks are sent from the hatchery to the Farmer's Co-op. O'mamma buys some and puts them in a cardboard box. Instead of a mother hen, they have a special light shining on them all day and night to keep them warm. Also, they need shavings under their feet, special chick food, and chick grit for digestion.

They are kept in the mudroom next to the kitchen. We like having them near us under the same roof so we can hear their happy peeping sounds before they learn to squawk.

Within a couple of weeks, the box is crowded because they've grown so much bigger. O'mamma drags a large metal trough into the laundry room and puts newspaper at the bottom with shavings on top. They still have the heat lamp on at night. Every day, she changes the bedding and gives them fresh food and water.

After two months, they've grown sturdy enough to survive living outside in the henhouse. At four months old, the hens are ready to lay eggs.

O'mamma knows how important it is to close and latch the henhouse door at night because, as she says, "Everybody likes chicken!" Her heart still sinks when she remembers the morning she opened the door to the coop too early, near dawn. The weasel came through, and we lost a hen. After that, she waited until mid-morning to re-open it and let them out.

The arrival of rats is an entirely different story. No work is involved in acquiring a whole pack because on their own they seek out places to live where it's safe and easy to get food. They try to avoid moving into a barn with cats, but sapiens have cats living in their barns to keep the rats out. Apparently, they don't understand how unwelcome they are.

The night the rats slipped in, our cats missed out on an important chance to be admired by Mr. Cliff for stopping the worst event of the year. They must have slept through the arrival of a pack of at least twenty. He said they didn't have anything to lose if they didn't do their job because no one in the cat group ate eggs.

I've never seen them do anything that looked like work, unless scowling counts. And watching rats run isn't doing a job. Watching is only a part of guarding, and that's my job!

According to Mr. Cliff, cats don't concentrate like he and I do. He called them Self-Centered Pleasure-Seekers (SC-PS). "We are reliable because we care, and cats are not because they do not." I guess it was their work ethic, not them, that made him scowl. But, I have never seen him stoop to pet one.

He was so angry they allowed the pack to slip past them that he said things I found hard to believe. "Rats amuse cats, so they don't even mind if they are around or not. Watching rats is only a hobby for cats!"

Day after day, we saw the rats live their silly little lives running around at the old barn. Chewing up stuff is what they did for work. Rat-bite marks were on the wood handles of every tool in there. And then there were the rat holes they made for secret passageways.

Worst of all was how they acted toward us. They didn't look anybody in the eye or try to communicate, and they didn't care about smelling awful. One would disappear right before your eyes and jump out of a rat hole behind you.

I didn't like being taken by surprise like that, and I let them know. Every time I saw one standing still, I'd say, *"You're not funny. You're rude and immature!"*

We hadn't ever known what it was like to fight for our own food before this generation arrived. Since they began stealing eggs as soon as they could and since the chickens had just started working again after their winter break, there were no eggs available for us. Breakfast wasn't the same tasty meal without egg leftovers for Pristine and me.

Last year was different. The rats who lived here then were so busy watching for their enemy Snake they had to focus on staying alive. As busy as that kept them, there wasn't much time to eat a lot of eggs. Not this year. On the first day of egg season, in a blink the whole pack switched from survival mode to self-indulgence.

Did the rats give any thought to our hungry longings for eggs? No, they did not!

Did they understand if they ate all of them, we would have none? No, of course not!

Mr. Cliff said they had a bad brain problem called No Perspective (NP). He said, "They don't understand how their behavior affects us because NP makes them dumb and selfish, too." I had seen that up close and too personally, so I agreed. Then he said, "I've seen sapiens with NP, too."

"What about canines?" I thought, but I didn't ask.

Part 2: Game Plan

To change this terribly unfair situation, O'mamma thought up a plan called "Beat the Rat." It sounded like a game. I guess it might have been, but not the fun kind. There were two sets of players, us and the rats. The winners were the first team to touch the egg immediately after the chicken laid it in the nest.

O'mamma decided to participate because at first she wasn't prepared to do anything else to solve our egg problem. It was her "best last choice" she said. I didn't understand what she meant.

The game went like this. Early in the morning O'mamma put out Laying Formula and fresh water for the hens. They pecked around, ate a little, cleaned up the spilled corn, and clucked to each other. They sang happily with cheerful trills and, on occasion, squawked a few complaints. O'mamma said they reminded her of housewives visiting over morning coffee before daytime TV got popular.

Mr. Cliff had made six nesting boxes, but for some hard to understand reason, they all wanted to lay their eggs in the same one. While one was sitting on what he called "the nest of the day," others would walk fast around the yard. A few stood still staring at the one on the nest.

Mr. C. didn't talk to animals much. I think frustration drove him to say, "Why did I build six when you all want to lay your eggs in one? I have never understood girls!"

Egg-laying looked like a high-pressure occupation to me. When the time came for the egg to arrive, the hen hurried to sit on a nest and wait. Often, a few hens got to the end of their patience waiting for another hen's egg to arrive. Hoping to force the sitting hen to hurry and move off the nest, they'd run back and forth in front of her squawking.

Once I saw a mad hen jump into the nesting box with someone already in there. Hen-on-Hen was uglier than a rooster fight. All that pecking and scratching and squawking made it look scary. There weren't any rules. Now when feathers fly, I turn away and run to the house.

As soon as she laid her egg, the hen jumped off the nest. Then, she strutted around the coop and into the yard cackling as loudly as she could. That was the signal for both the rats and O'mamma to start the race.

Game on! The two sets of running players came from opposite directions. The rats had been hanging around the barn chewing on wood, waiting for food to be delivered to them, even more evidence of having No Perspective.

O'mamma was in the house writing. At the sound of the signal, she threw open the back door and ran across the yard toward the egg. The rats left their wood and ran too.

As she ran, she hollered my name, "Arr-thurr!"

They were faster. By the time we got there, a few of them were already sitting in the nesting box eating the egg.

I felt like they were laughing at us, but I didn't want her to know. She did realize they had an unfair advantage, four legs instead of her two. And they could take shortcuts through the holes they had chewed in the floor and the walls.

Not that it would have made a big difference, but in my opinion, she should have thrown away those "crocs" and worn running shoes. I told her, *"Crocs are named for crocodiles because they cover ground fast, but running shoes don't eat anything."* Wow! That sounded crazy!

"This game is driving me out of my mind. I wish I could help O'mamma find another way to get our eggs and stop the madness before she and I lose what sanity we have left."

She regretted making a plan so awful for us. I felt bad, too. A game that was so unfair was called one-sided. No game was fun when only one side had a chance to win. You had to stop playing, or you wouldn't stop feeling bad.

I had another wild thought, and it wasn't crazy. *"We have gotten caught in our own home-made rat trap!"*

Even though we never won, we had no choice but to keep playing.

O'mamma wasn't sure what to do to get out of the predicament, so she did what she always does at a time like this. She thinks. After she thinks for a while, she makes a list.

That's what she did. Here was her list:

*Objectives: Get rid of rats. Secure eggs.

*Experience: I have trapped cats, mice, possum, and rats successfully before.

Options: *Rating—Bad or Good:*
  1. Starve rats -relocate chickens and food
                      1. Too much trouble—bad
  2. Capture and remove
                      2. Worked well before—good
  3. Kill and remove
                      3. Only for diseases—N/A, bad

Equipment:
  1. Traps—humane
  2. Gloves—bite proof
  3. Bait—peanut butter or cat food
  4. Rat poison—optional for emergency use only
  5. Transportation—truck, gas

6. Destination—map for choosing drop off point

7. Bravery—one whole nerve pill

In only one hour we had a Capture/Remove/ Relocate Plan. O'mamma told Mr. Cliff that a solid plan was just as calming as a nerve pill. And we didn't need the poison either.

Oh-oh! No peanut butter. Oh well, the cats wouldn't miss one can of food. The rest of the list had things on it we kept as standard equipment.

A few hours later, I heard the Relocation phase of the plan was in progress. I quickly decided that it wasn't wise for me to leave the farm unguarded for several hours.

Besides that, the disturbing image of unhappy rats climbing over one another and staring at me with their beady eyes was one of those things that would have haunted me in my dreams. Allowing myself to see that would have been contrary to the guiding principle of my most important mantra, Nothing-shall-spoil-the-pleasure-of-napping.

As the plan went forward, I was uncomfortable. I wondered if I should feel guilty for not going, so I made myself wait at a ComfLev4 station on gravel.

A few hours later O'mamma and Mr. Cliff returned. They talked about how satisfied they were with the new location. It was somewhere south, on twelve hundred acres of woods and uncut fields, near a stream and an abandoned barn. Perfect!

Worries

Part 1: On the Passion Express

A few days ago, O'mamma was complaining fast and loud, as loud as a shout about something or other. Mr. Cliff wanted to know what was going on. "I am expressing myself with the passion of opera singers," she declared indignantly.

Really? I was there. It sounded ordinary, not at all artistic. At least she wasn't singing. But like me, Mr. Cliff knew what it was about. A huge branch from the fifty-foot cedar tree had fallen on her car and cracked the windshield last week. She'd been cleaning up the mess it left ever since.

"You're expressing your feelings. That's okay. We all complain when bad things happen." He was trying to soothe her with gentle, understanding words. "Under the circumstances, you should have the right to shout as loud as you want. We understand." I disagreed.

"Speak for yourself. I'm the one with sensitive ears. There are many ways to complain without disturbing everyone.

"Move your eyes side to side. Give a big sigh. Sometimes, I lower my head and gaze upward, or I bring my tail down. Even a slight display of cuspid and a low growl can work.

"There's no need to let the neighbors in on the details of what they already suspect."

Mr. Cliff took it one step further. He told her he had decided to change the word "complaining" to "Passionate Expression" for times when anyone in our family voiced honest distress. That way, O'mamma wouldn't be the only one who would be free to shout, or even howl, about how bad they felt. He hoped she might like what he said because she could feel like he approved of her style. Maybe, it would help the next time something upset her.

"That's kind of him," I thought, but I wondered if my big guy might be going too far and really just be trying for personal credit. Gentle soothing to calm "the passion of opera singers*"* was a long shot.

Then in a blink, he surprised us by switching over to teasing. "You're on the Passion Express!" He laughed, but she didn't. At times like this, I knew I'd never understand the mind of man.

O'mamma became upset again yesterday. She walked fast through the house. From the living room to the sun porch, past the dining area and library, and back around again she talked to herself out loud, too loud. Mr. Cliff and I locked eyes. Both of us knew... she was on the Passion Express.

"I have never ever worried about the right thing!" she shouted. "All that time worrying about things that never happened was wasted. Fires, floods, fevers, and now falling trees are what actually happened. Why didn't I prepare for those? Duh-uh, I had filled my mind with the wrong catastrophes, that's why!"

"I had a balloon at the Thanksgiving Day Parade when I was seven. It was moving up and down with the breeze. I was afraid that the wind might take it away, so I pulled it close. Bang! The buckle on my black patent leather shoe had popped it. What a shock! I should have noticed then I was way off track when it came to knowing what the real dangers were."

Now she was shouting even louder. "I do not now and never have chosen the right thing to worry about. A Life-Changing Awareness, that's what this is!"

"Okay, slow down. I can't keep up when words come so fast and loud.

"You are saying... that you know now... you never worried about the right thing... because your mind was busy... with the wrong thing. So you believe knowing this will... change... your... life."

She continued, "If I don't know how to choose the right worry, why worry at all! It's a waste of time. It's a waste of energy. Instead, I could be outside smelling the roses."

To my surprise, the hair on my back stood up. My immediate response was passionate opposition to her declaration.

"Smelling the roses? Don't you remember you decided not to plant roses? If I chased a squirrel too close to a rose bush, you told me the thorns could pierce my skin.

"You said you would never put anything in the garden that had thorns. Are you going to go back on your word, stop caring, and plant roses?

"If you stop worrying, will that create safety problems for all of us?

"Is this Life-Changing Awareness about to change our lives, too?"

All those questions made me aware that worrying was a job. Suddenly, I realized that it's part of prevention which is part of protection! Now we needed someone else to do the job O'mamma always did. We had taken for granted that she'd continue worrying forever.

Who could take over? Not Mr. Cliff. Nothing seemed to make him worry except being deprived of empty calories.

Not me. My job was already full time. And for those who would say "I doubt that," I say, *"Napping is a necessary part of guarding. It recharges the batteries of the senses!"*

During the night there was a loud storm, the kind that scares a lot of us.

Part 2: Farrier Day

The new day was clear and cold. When we woke up, Mr. Cliff reached for his phone on the bedside table and looked at the weather report. He liked to lie on his back and announce the weather for what he called "the next twenty-four."

"Bundle up girls, it's chilly out there, thirty-nine degrees and falling tonight to twenty-two."

"No problem, Mr. C. I'm in your military story now where the top guys call the bottom guys 'girls.' We have that guy thing going."

At thirty-nine degrees, I always refused a coat if the sun was out. O'mamma and Pristine, the real girls, put their coats on and off to the barn we went.

First, the cats and horses needed to eat. Then, the floor where the farrier worked at shoeing had to be swept before he came later in the morning. After that, we'd go back to the house for honey toast.

While O'mamma was sweeping inside the barn, I ran along the perimeter of Misty Meadows near the sand arena and went under the fence to enjoy the night critters' scents in the park next door. I was sniffing along the trail singing "The Nose Knows Song."

"My eyes can't see it.
My ears can't hear it,
But my nose knows,
Nose knows."

I saw Gray Cat on her way to the barn. She looked over at me with that scowl, the No Respect Scowl. I haven't yet and never will get used to that look. It was hard to remain calm.

All the other cats before her used to notice how hard I worked to keep them safe. They felt great respect and admiration for my skill and dedication. That was obvious from the way they quickly moved aside as I passed. Yup, Pup, those were Tails-Up times!

I followed Gray Cat with my eyes narrowed. Repeating Cat Mantras didn't help me not lose complete control. I ran at her full speed across the arena kicking up sand as I went. She flew through the barn door first.

Usually, her flight path ended in a perfect landing on top of the refrigerator. This time, she couldn't get there because the door to the feed room was closed. I looked up at the eaves and along the rafters, but I couldn't see her. Where had she gone?

There was time for only the first blink of worry before O'mamma came toward me smiling. "Almost finished here, Arthur," she said.

My thoughts moved on to eating. No cat was going to cause the shadow of worry to follow me to the house for breakfast.

O'mamma fixed her tea. Pristine and I gathered around the table to share honey toast with her. We had just finished the Ceremony when I heard the sound of a vehicle on gravel. A truck was traveling across the yard toward the barn.

"He's already here! Let's go out. The farrier's here," she called to us.

His truck was a different kind of truck with doors on the sides that lifted up. The first time she saw it pull next to the barn, O'mamma mistook it for a food truck. Just in case the Mr. Lamplick might be selling hot dogs on the weekends, I investigated.

It wasn't true! There weren't any scents of food inside. The truck was filled with metal, iron horseshoes, tools, and the fire-making forge. The forge was for heating the iron shoes so they could be bent to fit Cody's feet.

As we approached, Mr. Lamplick was already firing it up. His helper rolled the hoof stand over to him in the shoeing area.

"Good morning. How are you doing?" O'mamma replied, "Pretty well, what about you?" That's how it always started off, nice and polite.

Then O'mamma heard, *"Meow.""*Where are you?" She was talking to both herself and the cat. "Oh, no, what are you doing up there? Maybe it was the storm last night that scared you into going up so high. Tonight the temperature will be falling to twenty-two degrees!

"Don't worry. We'll get you down because Mr. Lamplick is on his way. Remember, he's a fireman as well as a farrier, so he'll climb the barn ladder and be the hero who rescues our favorite cat!"

When Gray Cat couldn't land on the refrigerator, somehow she'd been able to use her claws to get all the way up the ten-foot wall to the wood storage loft over the rooms in the barn. Amazingly, I had scared her that much. She must have believed in my speed!

Was the No Respect Scowl only a bluff? All of a sudden, the Tails-Up feeling came back. If I could have, I would have smiled, but I was worried about O'mamma finding out the truth behind Gray Cat's predicament.

Mr. Lamplick had finished trimming Cody's hooves and nailed on new shoes. While his helper swept the hoof shavings into a pile, he packed up the forge and tools himself. He seemed impatient and grumpier than on other days.

Usually, they'd set a date for the next shoeing, O'mamma would pay him for his work, and then he'd leave. O'mamma wrote the check, but this time she told him she needed his help.

"The cat is up there, and I can't open the tall ladder. It's going to be below freezing tonight, only twenty-two degrees."

Walking toward the double sliding door of the barn without slowing down, he said, "Cats can find their own way down. Don't you worry about that, little lady."

Having no idea that using the words "worry" and "little lady" would cause a bold reaction, Mr. Lamplick was totally unprepared for her next move. He was striding toward the doorway but still inside the barn when she sprinted past him. She hugged the heavy closed ladder and swung it into his path saying, "Open this ladder for me, please sir!"

Shock made him stop short. She and the ladder were between him and the door. I thought I heard a low growl but no words came out as Mr. Lamplick struggled to open it.

O'mamma stepped aside satisfied. Mr. Lamplick, red-faced, rushed toward his truck, jumped in, and drove away so fast that the gravel from the drive flew in all directions. I watched in amazement.

"What kind of fireman wouldn't climb a ladder to save a cat? Their job is to save lives! I don't even like cats, but she is one of us.

"If it had been someone else in trouble, would he have said the same thing? What if it had been me?"

O'mamma knew I was upset. She said, "Arthur, we have no idea why he acted that way. He could have been in a terribly important rush, pressured to get somewhere. Maybe a barn full of horses was waiting to be shod before dark.

"And the fire department is big. Each fireman might have a specialized job. Mr. Lamplick may be the one who drives the truck and doesn't ever climb a ladder.

"I understand, and I feel bad too. It's sad that for the past seven years we thought we had a helper who cared about all of us. Everyone is not always who we'd like them to be.

"The fact is we have to handle our own problem. So it's better if we stick to saying we're disappointed and leave it at that.

"Let's put all of our energy into helping Gray Cat, okay?"

Part 3: Jump Kitty Jump

What will make her want to come to us? Let's think," O'mamma said. "Hmm... Cats love their beds and food. Hmm... I've got a plan. First, I need to get the ladder next to the wall."

With it in her arms like they were dancing, she tipped the ladder side to side and sang, "One, two, three... one, two, three." She moved it to the best spot and climbed to the top.

"Uh, oh, we're still three feet from being even with the loft floor."

Without explanation, O'mamma walked to the old barn and brought back several wooden boxes and boards. Up and down the ladder she went carrying them one by one, placing each piece carefully on the pile at the top on the ledge.

She disappeared into the feed room and came out smiling with Gray Cat's bed. "Almost ready!" she said climbing up again.

The bed was positioned on the boards and boxes and looked ready for Gray Cat to land in it. Oh, no! The pile still wasn't high enough to meet the level of the loft floor.

Gray Cat came to the edge and stared down at her bed. For a blink, O'mamma looked worried. Then, she spoke in a solemn voice sounding tougher than usual.

"You will have to jump. God helps them who help themselves, kitty. You've got to do your part."

"Yes, yes, yes!" I agreed with that. *"Do your part! Here, kitty, kitty."*

O'mamma balanced the cat bed on a single board she held with both hands and raised her arms as high as they would reach over her head. She stood on the top rung in that precarious position nine feet up from the concrete floor. Tilting the angle of her extended arms, she tried to get as close as possible to the edge of the loft. Her focus was on holding the board level and still, so "kitty" would make the jump safely.

She chanted slowly and in a one-two-three rhythm. "Jump, kitty, jump… jump, jump, jump! Jump, kitty, jump… jump, jump, jump!"

They stared at one another. Gray Cat understood and looked at her bed again. She slid one front paw down along the wall and leaned forward almost to the tipping point but stopped and retreated. Forward… retreat, forward… retreat.

Then, O'mamma herself retreated halfway down the ladder. She rested her arms, took a deep breath, and gave Gray Cat a long and gentle but serious look. Slowly, she climbed back up to the top. Once again holding the cat's bed balanced on the board over her head, O'mamma tilted it toward the edge of the loft floor.

Gray Cat returned to the edge and looked at her curiously. Calmly, she leaned forward, placed both front paws against the wall below her, and pushed off from above with her back feet. She flew through the air and landed in the bed!

In a blink, O'mamma lowered the board, bed, cat and all to the pile of boxes on top of the ladder. She grabbed Gray Cat by the scruff of her neck and held her close and tight. Likewise, Grey Cat clutched O'mamma's jacket digging into the fleece with her claws.

Step by step, they came down together with O'mamma chanting in a steady rhythm "I said, 'Jump, kitty, jump,' and she landed in her bed. I said, 'Jump, kitty, jump,' and she landed in her bed."

"Sure, she jumped, and she landed. Big deal! Cats do that every day.

"Wow, wow, wow."

So much celebration over one cat jump irritated me. My expression let everyone know my attitude had soured. I was unhappy that all the work of rescuing Gray Cat might end up increasing her popularity and propelling her into a new career.

"This could be the start of something big, something like the debut of a female feline star who found fame flying through the air at Misty Meadows Farm. Wow, wow, wow!" Sour had turned to bitter.

Later in the day I looked back and saw that thought was far-fetched. It had come out of my own insecurities. O'mamma was busy being ecstatic, gleefully reveling in the successful rescue of her beloved cat, and I was busy being jealous.

"We all worked together, and she did it! She understood what to do. Gray Cat trusted us! She cooperated!

"Trusting and cooperating are natural for us but very difficult for a cat. Thank you for helping and staying calm, Arthur."

O'mamma has a way of making us all feel important no matter what kind of contribution we make. Even so, it was hard for me to have confidence in my importance to her while someone else was getting the praise I longed to hear.

Softly to myself I repeated the things she had said to me. If I heard them again, I'd feel good one more time. *"We all worked together. Thank you for helping and staying calm, Arthur."*

Sigh...

Two Cat Mantras
(to be chanted rhythmically)

CAT-TROUBLE

Cats are trouble.
We agree. We agree.
Cats are trouble,
Says O'mamma to me.
No scaring, no chasing.
I agree. I agree.
Cats can make trouble
For O'mamma and me.

ONE-CAT-TWO

Oh, there's a cat.
Oh no, there're two.
If you look at them,
They'll look at you
You'll be mad,
And you'll be sad
When they make you do
What you know you shouldn't do.

LEG MAN

Part 1: In The One Cane Days

In the old days when I was young, Mr. Cliff and I spent hours together. He had retired from managing tall buildings, and O'mamma worked in an office not too far from Misty Meadows. On a day off once in a while, she'd take me out for a ride to new places.

Lately, she's been telling him about some of our trips, like the first time she took me to a vet's office. That happened only a few days after I arrived.

At the clinic, I sat on her lap while we waited in a tiny room. Dr. Bell walked in and smiled. I could tell that his heart melted when he saw me. He picked me up and lifted me over his head like I was the best new arrival. "He's just a little baby," he said. I could feel the tender strength of his hands as he held me, so I wasn't one bit afraid. After that, I was always happy to see him again.

Mr. Cliff's been sharing his memories of work he and I did together outside around the farm and of relaxing inside in front of the TV. Because he took me along with him on the tractor, I saw the barn and fields from all angles. He watched me grow, and now he calls what he saw "his story," my story. But it's his story, too.

"You were on earth for only twelve weeks when you came to live at Misty Meadows," Mr. C. said when he looked back. One time, he added that he had been here for three thousand, six hundred and forty since he was born. O'mamma has never mentioned her number of weeks or years either.

Recalling how tiny I was and how large everything else seemed was fun for them. It all looked huge to me too, except for my puppy-size bed and bowl. I tried to see the whole barn by moving my head up and down and side to side. For big things like the barn and the house, the tractor, and tall sapiens like Mr. Cliff, it took a lot of effort to get the whole picture.

Then I met the horses. They were beyond big even bigger than enormous. Humongous is the word I would use now. Every time they galloped past us, the ground rumbled. That scared me. Mr. Cliff could tell because I would try to hide behind his legs. For a long time whenever the horses came our way, he would say "Get over here near me, R.T.!"

When I did, I was close enough to see he had a problem with walking. One leg worked like it should and the other one didn't. At first, he used just one cane on the opposite side of the leg with the problem. When I walked with him, I purposely chose the side near the ankle that couldn't bend. That way, I showed how protective I wanted to be.

As it turned out, I'd also chosen for myself without even trying. Actually, it was safer over on my side because of how he used his cane in his conversations with the world.

When Mr. Cliff felt something, his vigorous energy went at the speed of light down his right arm through his hand. The cane came to life, and they became a team delivering his message. I watched as he made the cane dance around his legs in the rhythm of his words. It was hard to decide which one was more eloquent, the cane or him.

In order to show exactly what he wanted the world to know, he held the cane in different positions. With a big smile appearing on his face, he'd twirl the cane around his hand backward in clockwise circles. And when he whistled, I knew he was extra happy, even jubilant.

If something frustrated him, his hand grabbed the cane in the middle. Then, he threw it up and down and stomped it on the ground two times. Thump! Thump! Just in case he might have been upset with me, I lowered my tail and my ears to show respect. That seemed to help him relax because he knew he had me on his side.

While making an important point and feeling like no one was paying attention to it, or to him, he held his arm straight out, tossed the cane into the air, and caught it as it fell. Moving it up and down and side to side, he made the shape of a cross to the beat of what he was saying. If you'd been there to see it, you might have heard the music of a band following their leader and seen hundreds of pairs of feet marching to the cadence of his speech.

For a "yonder" story and for giving directions, he held the cane by the crook steady and straight out like a long, pointing finger. All you had to do was to let your eyes follow along its length to the black rubber tip. Going past the tip and straight ahead, BAM!, your eyes landed on the very thing he wanted you to see.

Proudly and straight from the heart, I like to say that I walk with a powerful man, a dramatic man who expresses himself as well a President or, even better than that, as well as the guy who stars in movies we watch, a man named Clint!

If a metal stick with a rubber tip can rise up to become the communications assistant for someone so admirable, who knows what level I might get to. Even though I consider that cane lucky, honestly, I wouldn't want its job with anyone but Mr. Cliff. Moods change dangerously fast in the important and even faster in the self-important.

Privately, I reassured myself that it's been better to stay on as a Farm Manager solving high-profile protection problems. After all, a lot of my time guarding has been spent lying on ComfLev1 beds.

I have the goal of being admired by my favorite man. I'm sure of that now, so I need to find something special, something more impressive than the daily work of guarding. I realize it might take a lot of effort and sacrifice.

The Incremental Person lesson we all learned from O'mamma is always in my mind. Every day, I give myself bit-by-bit advice for making it through the meantime.

"Slow down. Keep thinking and make a plan. Do the best job you can day by day at your current level. You will find a way."

If I don't give up, I know it will happen because where there is a will, there is a way.

Part 2: The Logic of Certain Powers

In the evenings while O'mamma cooked supper, Mr. Cliff and I had our "alone time." Yup, Pup, that's what sapiens called being together in a room. I was not alone, and he wasn't either.

"What's going on?" I asked myself. *"Is it me? Or are they saying something I'm too Doggone Dumb (DD) to understand?"*

Whenever I heard what their minds came up with and the words they chose that didn't make sense, I wanted to howl. I had no idea that in just a few blinks the Sapiens Not Making Sense Factor (SNMSF) would make my head spin worse than it ever had before.

"Ring... ring. Ring... ring." Who was calling Mr. C's phone? Why so near supper time? I didn't welcome our togetherness being interrupted by a third party.

"Encroachment! Ten-minute penalty!" I howled. I knew I sounded bitter, but I was hungry.

"Oh, please, not Charlie again!"

They talked and laughed while I lay there in the shadow of the lamp having true alone time. As whiff after whiff of delicious smells of food cooking floated in from the kitchen, it got harder to ignore the hunger pangs.

I didn't know what Charlie said, but Mr. Cliff laughed and said, "I'm a leg man."

"*What's a leg man?*" I sat up and raised my nose as high in the air as possible. Had I missed something? Was fried chicken on the menu tonight?

Then, I remembered another friend of his who protected fighter pilots in battles with enemy planes. That guy was called a "wing man."

I decided quickly, too quickly it turned out, that their conversation had to be about either 1) Naval Aviation in the Korean Conflict or 2) fried chicken. But which one was it?

While I was struggling to solve the meaning of the irritating word conundrum, I recognized that I had brought it on myself by eavesdropping.

"*Maybe it's a crime, and I'm being punished for it,*" I thought.

"*No, silly boy, you're just hungry.*"

"*Okay,*" I said to my inner voice, "*and thank you.*"

What happened next changed the entire direction of my investigative imagination. Mr. Cliff shifted his legs on the recliner extension and accidentally kicked the blue metal canes leaning against the side table. They tumbled across one another and fell to the ground making a ruckus.

I remembered Mr. Cliff using one cane. Its name was "My Cane." He often misplaced that one. Scowling as he looked for it, he would mumble "Where's My Cane?" Then, he decided that two was a better idea for balance. He called the pair Cane and Able after two brothers in the Bible.

"Two canes, hmm... Two legs, hmm..." My mind was beginning to travel along a promising new line of thought.

I pictured Mr. Cliff walking toward me. Using two canes and two legs to move forward worked the same as having four legs. I knew I was getting closer to the answer I needed when I pictured Charlie standing on only two legs.

The longer I mulled it over, the more sure I was that the answer was rushing my way. A sudden brain surge made me shout, *"It's all about competition!*

"A smooth and logical path is finally mine to follow. It's just like horsepower in a car," I reasoned. *"The power that makes vehicles of all kinds move is counted by how many horses are there even though you can't see them. The more there are, the more power you have, and the* faster *you can go.*

"Power from legs, even cane legs, can be measured *that way too. Ha! Sounds right to me, so what more can I say!"*

The truth of the lie ended up being that horse-power and leg-power weren't really lies but exactly the same type of illusion. And both were created by male minds that enjoyed counting, measuring, and competition.

Guys wanted to be known as the fastest and strongest because a reputation like that helped them get the most attention and actually the most of everything else.

So Mr. Cliff, by calling himself a "leg man," was reminding Charlie that counting his canes as legs brought him double the power of two regular legs. And he was feeling double special just thinking about it.

"Time for a Celebration Mantra for our Special Leg Man!!"

THE-DOUBLE-SPECIAL-MANTRA

First, Say it slow-ly
Ro-l-l it off your tongue.
Dou-ble Spec-ial
Spe-cial Spe-cial
Dou-ble Special
Spe-cial Spe-cial

Twice as fast
Chant it now
Special Special
Double Special
Special Special
Double Special.

"Ha! Ha! Ha! See how much fun it is when you jump in and get the feeling. That's what special is really all about... Having Fun and Feeling Great!"

Part 3: On The Way to the A-List

The great feeling lasted for a few weeks. Mr. Cliff and I continued to spend our "alone time" in the living room just the same as before his victory over Charlie. The longing for admiration from him continued to hover over my spirit. I still hadn't figured out a plan.

I wondered if there was another man Mr. Cliff admired. *"Why not ask?"* I thought.

"Harold," he said.

"Harold, the kid who wants to go to Mars!" I didn't hold back my shock.

Harold began working here when he was young, only fourteen. Mr. Cliff spent an hour a day with him, five days a week for four years. Harold grew strong by lifting hay bales and cleaning up. Running with the track team made him even stronger. By the time he left for college he was grown, a young man. Mr. Cliff was proud of Harold. Like me, he had a king's name.

From what I could tell they talked just about as much as guys did while they were working. Harold sounded really smart to me. He said that school was easy and that he liked studying math.

O'mamma agreed that he was very intelligent. She wrote a letter recommending he become a member of the Honor Society in his school. Last fall, he went to college to study more things so he can go to Mars someday. When the ship is ready, he will be too.

After Harold left, O'mamma hung the Farm Help Needed sign on the fence between us and the park. Sapiens who like to walk and run outdoors pass by. Some have dogs, and some stop to talk to our horses. In only a few hours, Stuart called. He was walking with Chuck his wife's yellow lab like he did every day.

"Hey, I see your sign," he said. "I grew up on a farm in Minnesota. I'd like to help you out. Chuck is good with horses so he could come with me and run off-leash. He'd like that!"

Mr. Cliff told him to stop by and meet us. So we met, and all liked each other. I thought Chuck was a decent sort of canine, steady with no obviously aggravating habits.

The same routine went on with Stu as with Harold... an hour a day, five days a week. They had been men for so long they had a lot to tell one another. Mr. Cliff told all kinds of stories I'd already heard. Stu had new stories, mostly about Texas and his restaurant.

"How did you get to own a restaurant?" O'mamma asked.

"Well," he said, "It's kind of unusual how it happened. My wife and I went to this restaurant that had four dishes I liked. The owner decided to close up shop because he was tired. I was upset about losing my favorite food, so I bought him out.

"I told my wife I could cook because my mother made all five of her sons learn how. 'That way,' she said, 'I can rest easy knowing you'll always be able to fix yourself something to eat.' She was right. She never dreamed, though, I'd end of feeding people whose mothers didn't know boys could cook if you made them do it."

"But in a restaurant, there's a menu of so many kinds of dishes. How did you know what to do?" O'mamma was in awe of his courage to take on a responsibility so huge and with something he never had done before.

"I studied," Stu replied. "I took classes and read cookbooks to learn what flavors tasted good with others. Some things got baked, and some needed to be fried to taste good like okra. I studied quite a bit until I knew what to do about making up a menu."

"What happened to the restaurant?" she asked.

"Well, cooking is hard work. And it's not only the food preparation. Someone has to clean, and order supplies, as well as take care of the money and so many other things. I didn't mind hard work, but I needed to hire people to work with me.

"On the farm, my father had sons who helped him. We all pitched in. I was used to that. But hiring people who wanted to pitch in wasn't so simple. I found that part more tiring than working. So after a few years, I sold out."

After he finished talking, my mind wandered back to the other guys who had made it to the List of Admired Men.

"Eureka! I have discovered something. They all did the same thing... study, study, and study."

Clint studied acting. Mr. Cliff said so. And Stuart studied cooking. He said so. Harold studied math. He *and* his mother said so. Every man on the list studied something different. It wasn't *what* they studied. It was *that* they studied.

"What about me?" I thought. *"I'm on guard duty night and day. A half hour is all I'd have for it."*

Suddenly, I realized that I didn't have to go anywhere else to study because I could study legs while I was guarding! I worked in the midst of them. They walked, ran, and jumped past me every day. Mine went past them, too.

Nothing could be more perfect! Yup, Pup, I was on my way to the A-List. *"Someday, I'll be known as Arthur Dogson Todd, Leg Man, and Number One on Mr. Cliff's A-List!"*

Part 4: Study, Study, Study

E xcited about my plan, I strutted toward the barn singing a new song:

> *"Legs are all around me*
> *From the rafters to the floor*
> *Paws and claws surround me*
> *On two-leggers and on four"*

"*Life experience should count,*" I thought. "*After all, my legs have been moving alongside theirs for years. I've seen a lot from the so-so to the lovely.*

"*Maybe I know more than I think I do. Should I already consider myself a Leg Man?*

"*No, there's always more to learn, and I'll get extra credit for extra knowledge.*"

As a youngster, I chased everyone in sight without giving much thought to it. The horses' legs moved at an incredible speed. I lived for the thrill of running at their heels, weaving in and out, and barking as we crossed the fields. The sheer joy and adrenalin-laced terror propelled me forward.

Mr. Cliff said proudly that my superb speed and natural instincts kept me alive. O'mamma celebrated my abilities by making a long paper banner for the wall over the horse stalls in the barn. In large black lettering like a newspaper it read, "Twenty Pounder Makes Thousand-Pounders Run." *Ha! Ha!* I liked how it looked, and it sounded like true news because it was.

I was confident that I could keep up with the rhythm of horses' legs at the gallop well enough to be safe, but... One day in a blink I missed a beat, and my faltering caused Zip to step on my back leg.

Dr. Bell put a snug wrap on it and said I had to be "confined." For a month, I didn't run. All I could do was nap on the inside beds. Time went by slowly.

When I returned to duty, I joyfully approached Zip and Cody in the pasture. They stood still looking at me skeptically. My month-long absence had given them time to reconsider our relationship.

Being older and wiser, they were tired of being pressured to run if they didn't want to. It also might have been true that they were afraid of hurting me again.

Instead of running with me, they wandered around on their stocky, sturdy horse legs looking content. Sure, they had a few exuberant bursts of speed, but that wasn't nearly enough of a challenge for the daredevil I had become.

I tried to coax them politely, but I felt like an annoying insect bugging them. I didn't want to leave them out of playing just because they were getting old. I hope I'm not left out when I'm old.

So I ended up limiting myself to circling their heads and barking as they grazed. All that got me was two horses who shook their heads like a fly had landed.

Yes, it was true. They were treating me like an annoying insect. It's so sad, I thought, that a kind deed can be so misunderstood. *Sigh...*

Fortunately, O'mamma invited a new horse to live with us. A filly called Lace arrived and immediately made a five-foot-ten-inch jump out of the arena. Her legs were like tightly wound springs. Yup, Pup, she was a serious challenge for O'mamma, as well as Cody and Zip. To my joy, the fancy footwork resumed.

At only two years old this Nervous Nelly of a Morgan ran faster than the guys ever did. Her legs were beautiful, long, and slender with black hoof walls on large cupped feet. At a trot, she stepped high like a carriage horse.

She read me right when we played the Power-Over Game. I barely held my own, but I had one move she couldn't keep up with, a sharp turn to the right at full speed. After she saw my first few successful turns, there was a slight hint of hormonal spite in some of the counter-moves she made. Was she jealous of my skill?

Jealousy can be a problem, but it can also be flattering. We got past that, and our competition became a lot of fun.

The next group, the "Little-Furry-Purry-Loves" group, was hard to study safely. O'mamma called them that without having any idea that cats actually could be dangerous. They were just too cute and too sweet when she was nearby, but they gave me piercing stares when she wasn't. I'd been feeling uncertain about my safety around them for a while.

Then, I remembered I had heard something said about "going to the dogs" but nothing ever about "going to the cats."

"Why?" I asked myself. "If everyone knows sapiens have survived going to the dogs, why is there no information about anyone who went to the cats? Are there no survivors?"

I decided a little reassurance was in order. I stayed calm and said, "Don't panic. Approach slowly. You are going to the cats, uncharted territory."

The first time I saw cats, I was only three months old. Sammi and Fiona were years older than me, seven for Sammi and two for Fiona. They'd been adopted together from Animal Control before I arrived.

Sammi had been a parlor cat in a house for six years, but tragically, she had to move out because she made her family wheeze. At Misty Meadows, she became "Queen of the Barn."

The adoption counselor said even though O'mamma put two upholstered chairs and a side table in the heated cat room, there would be "a period of adjustment." The adjustment actually made was by everyone else because Sammi stayed annoyed for the next twelve years.

Fiona didn't "work out" O'mamma was told. She was too "natural" for an apartment. She followed her inherited cat instincts and wasn't interested in the price of inside life, domestication.

The counselor said she scratched the walls and furniture, jumped with great agility anywhere she chose, and didn't come when she heard, "Here kitty, kitty." Her owners said she was brain-damaged.

Since she stayed hidden in the hay stacked in two of the stalls, I didn't meet her until a year later. Over the next four years, she appeared more and more often and watched us work from high up in the eaves of the barn. Finally, she allowed O'mamma to pet her. After that, her favorite place to relax was on top of a hay bale out in the open.

Gray Cat, first called Angel, came at Christmas seven years ago. She was living under a nice woman's porch. O'mamma's friends Bethany and Bev trapped her so she could be brought to a more secure home. Sammi and Fiona would not welcome her to their territory, so Gray Cat also slept in the hay-bale stalls and watched us from high places.

Recently, after the other two passed on and she was the only one left, she moved into the cat room. O'mamma decided "the only feline on the premises" had been here long enough to deserve to have a room to herself. She's still the only cat living here. And that is fine with me!

Until this study, I didn't pay much attention to any of the cats unless they gave me the No Respect Scowl. Occasionally, we'd cross paths, and they'd scamper away. After a while I began to notice as soon as one got about four feet from me, she'd stop to turn and eye me from a crouched position.

I wondered, *"Do I look smaller from afar? Could I be mistaken for a mouse?"* It made me uneasy, but things moved fast on my job, so I just kept going where I was headed.

To complete the study, I needed to get closer to them. Instead of running, I began standing still when they paused and turned toward me. I would watch as their legs stiffened, and their bodies rose up into a hunched position ready to spring forward in a blink.

"Okay, stay calm, this is what danger looks like," I said. *"Remember, in one blink they can be in position to pounce."*

The tension grew as I got closer to my goal of being on the A-List. I felt the same excitement as when I first chased squirrels. I realized I'd outgrown that, and now I was chasing knowledge.

In the cats' room, I spotted a subject close enough to study. Sammi was lounging on her favorite upholstered chair, the brown and orange patterned one. I paused to appreciate the beauty of the scene.

"Her calico fur blends with the colors of the chair nicely," I thought. Not concentrating on imminent danger like I should have been, I advanced too far forward. There I was, standing way too close, so close that my eyes were even with the height of the chair seat.

All four of Sammi's legs lengthened as she stretched them toward me. Oh, no! Something strange-looking was emerging from each toe on every paw. I was paralyzed by the sight of cat claws up close. Not normal toenails like I have, these were weapons, curled, pointy, and sharp, two inches from my face. All eighteen of them were moving toward my nose in the horror of a slow-motion, inescapable moment.

It occurred to me that the price of knowledge might be too high. So I closed my eyes and slowly retreated. After taking a few steps back and a deep breath, I ran.

I worried that the scope of my study of cat legs was limited, but I could honestly blame it on their personalities. Every time I bravely moved forward to get a good look, I was threatened by subtle suggestions of physical harm. The tricky part was to reassure them that I wasn't a threat at the same time I moved forward to observe.

Enough, I was satisfied I had seen enough to understand as much as I possibly could about cat legs. So I wrapped up the cat portion of the study of legs with this final statement.

"For safety, the information gathered may omit some of the finer details of the physical bodies of cats. That's because I found their behavior difficult to navigate comfortably from less than three feet away. In regard to personality characteristics, the most important information is best stated this way. The insecure are hard to get to know."

The next and last group was the two-leggers. Sapiens would be easy because I'd already investigated Mr. Cliff's leg problem and his extras, the canes. I was familiar with those details, and so there was nothing more to add.

The same was true for O'mamma's legs because I'd been around her for years, and she walked with no problem. I was used to seeing her stride across the yard and barnyard. In the fields, she lifted her legs high up and over the tall grass like she was marching. And with Cody and Lace, she enjoyed running in the sand arena. Like other sapiens, she wore shoes or boots outside.

I never approved of those crocs she wore that made her lose the race with the rats. Recently, she finally bought a pair of running shoes.

Poultry, usually called chickens, or hens and roosters, had two legs but that was a very, very unattractive picture. Although it was difficult to describe, I was able to do my best by sticking to the facts. A nonjudgmental description was also the most kind because, after all, they couldn't help it.

They started out cute as chicks, but that's because all you could see was pre-feather "fur," called "down." By the time chickens were fully grown, their legs had bumpy skin and crooked, scaly feet. It was like looking at a regular bird wearing yellow frog-skin tights.

Three long toes in front with one to balance on the back were used for scratching to uncover bugs and seeds. The back toes had claws, and in addition, roosters had spurs part way up the back of their legs.

O'mamma labeled them "functional." I heard O'mamma say that when things were functional, pretty wasn't necessary. "It's more important to be able to find food than to be beautiful, and anyway, their pictures have sold as many calendars as baby pictures."

Overall, O'mamma said she enjoyed how beautiful hens and roosters looked after she had learned to disregard the unattractive parts.

"Wait a cock-crowing minute!

"Did I hear them talking about poultry legs at the exact same time I was studying them?"

Immediately, I remembered the conclusion I'd drawn a long time ago about coincidences... there aren't any.

"This is about me! They have been following my progress from group to group." I listened to every word that evening instead of napping.

"Arthur is through with his study," O'mamma said.

"I know," replied Mr. Cliff. "And I am proud of how dedicated he was to becoming an expert like me. His name is definitely going at the top of my A-List. I admire him. He's a true Leg Man."

O'mamma looked in my direction and asked, "Did you hear that Arthur? You have proven yourself to be a dedicated expert on legs by studying as hard as you did. You are now Number One on Mr. Cliff's List of Most Admired Men."

All I could say was, *"Where there's a will, there's a way!"*

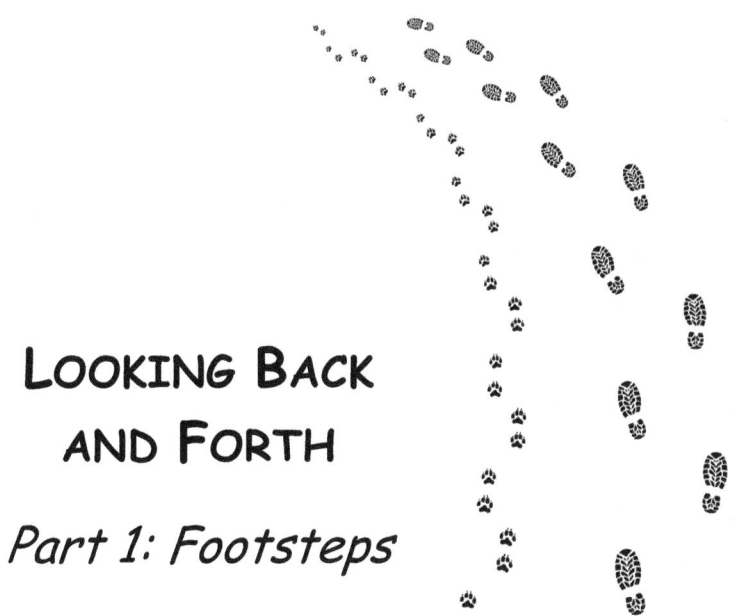

Looking Back and Forth

Part 1: Footsteps

The world I came to call My Forever Home was filled with great places for fun and adventure. There were the fields and hills where I ran with the horses, squirrels, and the others I chased, the pond for cooling off, and guarding beds to lie on in the winter sun or the shade from trees in summer. Mr. Cliff called me "a little guy in a great, big world."

While I was finding my way to maturity, I became an astute observer of "what was what" as Mr. Cliff called everything I eventually understood. Starting out at only three months old, I was too young to know what growing was about. I didn't realize I was actually learning or that I was working either. I just followed the flow of the day.

At first, I went everywhere O'mamma did. It took me a long time to stay close enough to her to be really in her footsteps, probably until I got my first Harley D collar. I was two years old then, Mr. Cliff said.

In the course of doing daily chores, O'mamma and I traveled across most of the farm. We walked back and forth from the house to the barn, past the chicken coop, across the sand arena to the haymow, and up over the hill and down. How many steps was that? Ten thousand in a day wouldn't even be close. I didn't know numbers yet, or I might have counted.

Enjoying every moment, I moved along on pure instinct. Often on our daily path, I became distracted by something moving. From the beginning, I could tell the difference between the motion of a leaf in the wind and a living being going on its own, especially insects.

Hopping bugs were the best! Watching cave crickets jumping in random rhythms and directions challenged me to catch one. I was like a sapiens kid playing a new video game except there wasn't any screen. But there was danger in the grass. *"In a blink something might bite me on the nose,"* I thought. That's when I discovered my brave spirit.

Since my nose was usually close to the ground, I looked down more than up. I never took notice of flying insects until I saw a cat trying to catch a butterfly. She couldn't. I tried too, and I couldn't either. I'm still frustrated by anything that won't land on the ground where I can nab it.

Listening to O'mamma on our daily walks taught me how to observe and think at the same time. She would talk about what she saw, "Look, Arthur!" and what she smelled, "I smell a rat!" and what she heard, "Who is squawking now?" Also, she explained that Mother Nature was there too. Even though we couldn't see what made us hot or cold and wet or dry, we learned it was because she moved the sun, the air, and the clouds around in the sky.

The more footsteps O'mamma and I took together the more understanding I had of her. One day, I realized that she alone was in charge of deciding how to take care of everything, like the buildings, animals, food, routines, and even bad behavior. With really important things, she seemed to have a hard time being sure of herself.

I knew because we would start going off in one direction, and then we'd suddenly backtrack. O'mamma often stopped as fast as she changed her mind. In fact, she stopped so fast I'd run into her if I didn't stay alert.

One of her biggest decisions was which group to feed first—the horses, chickens, cats, or dogs. She said it came down to which one pressured her most. Pounds, one thousand per horse multiplied by three horses, won out over sheer numbers and noise, eighteen squawking four-pound hens and two-five pound roosters.

The main rooster was so disrespectful we dreaded getting close enough to feed him and his hens. I think that's the real reason O'mamma decided to leave them locked in the coop and feed the horses first.

She was uncomfortable with the possibility of being known as an "enemy" of the rooster. So, from a distance standing high up on the tractor seat, she proclaimed her decision about who would eat first.

"The horses are stronger. If there were ever temper tantrums over waiting too long for food, they would lose their good manners and kick the doors down. Then, they'd stampede over to the chicken house, step on a few of you, and eat all the Laying Formula!"

Pristine and I were happy about what she said and how she presented it, loudly and firmly. Not one of us would have voted to face those fowls first each morning. And we certainly didn't want the rooster to carry a grudge against O'mamma.

Big J said the rooster lived to fight, so he agreed that living in fear of his grudge would be a bad thing. He called him "That Bird" at first, but after he worked here a while, he renamed him "Who-Lee-Oh" after his uncle who was teaching Jujitsu classes.

Who-Lee, for short, treated all of us as if we were intruders in his territory. Mr. Cliff was convinced he was aware of the Tennessee law about standing your ground. He called the rooster "a dangerous rogue."

Even though Who-Lee wasn't strong enough to destroy his coop door with those scrawny legs, he was equipped to hurt us. One time he flew through the air at O'mamma with his spurs and claws ready to strike. Two feet up off the ground flapping and squawking, he had gone control-crazy. We all watched him trying to land on her and stupidly attempt to dominate the one who fed him.

She was wounded two times on her leg before she was willing to whack him with the long bamboo pole Big J had cut for her from the cane break. The rogue hit the ground and looked dead. O'mamma started crying. After a couple of minutes, he struggled to his feet and shook his head from side to side. We all ran. He was never "right in the head" again.

For a blink during the attack, I'd been afraid O'mamma was being wishy-washy. That would have been worse than indecisive because it was about a having a weak spirit. I understand now that she had a hesitant look on her face because of having to choose between self-defense and hurting one of us. It had been her tender side making her into a flimsy-looking person.

Back then she was who she still is, but I wasn't who I am now. I didn't understand as much. I hadn't walked as far.

Part 2: Fear, Joy, and Maturity

E very morning as we trudged across the farm, O'mamma looked at what needed to be done and praised us for our work from the day before. We learned two things, to have pride in what we had accomplished and how to make sensible decisions. That helped us have confidence our work would make the good kind of difference.

"Mother Nature should be included in our choices for health and safety," she said. We learned to pay attention to things like temperature. When it was cool, she allowed us to make bigger plans that took more energy and lasted for a longer time.

On a hot day, we were told to stay out of the sun, move more slowly, and stop for a drink whether we felt thirsty or not. If I had a free minute, I'd secretly run to the pond and take a quick dip. It fit in with the "let nature guide your choices" idea, so I knew it was okay.

On cool days, O'mamma brought Cody into the sand arena where he exercised by jumping barrels laid out in a row and by doing the Walk-Trot-Canter routine around her in circles. Then, they played like two horses would. She'd lean forward and make blowing sounds running a few steps toward him from the center of the circle. He'd answer her, blowing louder as he ran with his nose down close to the sand. If she jumped up, he would too with all four feet off the ground.

His blowing was so powerful it sounded like the fire in the hot-air balloon that floated over our barn lot sometimes. That thing always scared him and Lace into galloping to the back pasture. I knew why. The noise it made sounded exactly like his. He thought a flying horse was coming after him. If I saw a flying dog after me, I'd run, too!

Their play ended with O'mamma's signal to stop, turn, and face her. She'd lean forward bending her knees and turning her head and shoulders sideways. Cody understood. He'd stop, turn, and walk slowly to her. She'd stroke his forelock and say, "You can run longer than me, big guy."

Our horses were as different as Pristine and I were from one another. When O'mamma brought Lace into the arena, it didn't look like they were playing. She focused on remaining calm while doing simple exercises with her.

At two years old, Lace had come to Misty Meadows scared silly and wild. The first thing she did was jump over the four-foot fence, clearing it by almost another foot. Although we all were impressed by her spectacular ability, we wished she could have developed it by having fun instead of out of the fear she had as a filly.

To help Lace get past her problem with panic, O'mamma asked her to do things like stand still, walk a few steps, and stand still again. After she had mastered that drill, she learned the "Put Your Nose on It" game.

Lace was supposed to walk to a fencepost or gate, relax, and touch it with her nose. The next level of that exercise was to put her nose on something "scary," like a green barrel. I watched them for a while before I realized that a horse was being given treats for relaxing and nose-touching.

"How difficult can it be to breathe out instead of in? What about me?" I thought. *"I pant after running fast on the job."* I sounded disgruntled, but if breathing counted toward treats, I had missed out on too much of what I deserved.

Then, I remembered Lace's scary background as a filly. Being born with a swayback made her different. At her first home, she had been conditioned to live in fear because she was mistreated by other mares. If she had let herself relax, she wouldn't have been ready to run from the danger that was always there.

The instinct for self-preservation saved her life, but she didn't get to enjoy things she got so good at. She didn't learn to trust anyone either, so I guess she must have been lonely as well as scared.

Now, as Lace was improving with exercises, I admitted that I had been unkind when judged her as if she'd had the same safe early life as I did. I was wrong.

I was proud of Lace, but honestly, I was more proud of myself and my maturity. The fact was saying you're wrong was harder than standing still even though both might be scary.

O'mamma said my reward was her pride in me that I truly deserved, but it didn't sound anything like what I craved.

"At least throw in a few truck rides to the bank. I still like their doggy cookies." Ha! Ha!

I knew that I might have sounded immature, even silly, but I wanted what I said to deflect attention away from the seriousness of my newly found Truly Mature Values (TMV). I hadn't come out in the open about that yet.

I didn't agree with O'mamma on everything like I used to. A gap had grown between her and me. I believed her time management ways were wasteful. My own, stricter standards for efficiency and production developed as part of my more mature attitude. According to efficiency estimates I calculated, if she had done things my way, we would have accomplished more of the really important things. And I knew I wasn't totally wrong.

My complaint stemmed from O'mamma scheduling time on work days for relaxation and fun. Everyone but me enjoyed it. I told her it didn't suit my nature, and I refused to join in.

"Happy enthusiasm is irritating me," I said. Mr. Cliff overheard me. He talked to me privately and added an important point. "Happiness," he said, "has the power to

make all warm-blooded beings stronger physically and mentally."

Supposedly, it would give our spirits strength for use in future stressful times. I had a hard time listening since it wasn't what I believed. But as he talked on and on about it, I thought less about the words he was saying and more about the respect others had for his opinions.

Men admired his strength and thought he was a lot of fun too, so changing my mind made more sense than staying stubborn and alone. *"At least I should give it a try,"* I thought. If men would call me mature even though I was having fun on the job, I was all for it now.

I began to wonder about the men who thought he was strong. When they saw him and me together, did I look like I could be his son? I knew it was impossible, but I wished it weren't.

Sigh...

Part 3: And The Crowd Cheered

Soon after I allowed myself to believe that fun was good for building strength, I needed every bit I had for the stress of what happened next. An exciting adventure flew past us... horses gone wild... and we had to chase it.

We were relaxing in the yard right before our mood was propelled from calm to frantic in two blinks. Our three horses stood grazing behind the house when Zip spotted the gate in the white picket fence standing open.

He galloped through and across the front two acres toward the main gate with Cody and Lace following his lead. The vibrations from their thundering hooves and the sight of their mane flying as high as the tops of their heads made my heart pound. They passed through the front gate leaving Misty Meadows in a cloud of dust.

Zip made a sharp right turn and continued to run down the road to the driveway of the Methodist Church to the east of us. All three flew across the churchyard and ended up on the front lawn of the Rescue Squad Station next door.

There, they paused and calmly began to eat the short green grass. In half a blink they had changed from escapees on the run to horses lazily grazing. Crazy! It was crazy. They were standing still nibbling with their heads down as if they had been there since dawn.

A short road between the church and the Rescue Squad Station went on back to the Recycling Center. Sapiens driving along it toward the bins came to a sudden halt when they saw horses grazing near an ambulance.

"Whoa!" one man said, "We ain't so plumb country out here that horses git hitched to ambulances. What's goin' on?"

They parked their pickup trucks and cars. Some got out and watched. Some tried to help. A few ran toward the horses holding ropes. One came charging at them with a broom, another with a rake. An assistant from the equine hospital across the road arrived with leads and halters.

Our horses had drawn a crowd! And the escape had turned into a community event. Sapiens in the park ran and hoisted their children to the second board of the three plank fence between them and the commotion. We could hear sweet, little voices calling, "Here, horsey. Here, horsey."

As a group of round-up volunteers approached, the horses moved away slowly, still nibbling, until they were against the fence between our farm and the church. The volunteers had no idea that they could be seen closing in from behind. It didn't matter how careful they were. It's impossible to sneak up on a horse.

O'mamma looked panicked as Cody stirred. Suddenly he bolted past everyone and headed for the main road.

To the amazement of all watching, he made two sharp left turns onto the road and into our driveway.

Zip and Lace followed running and bucking in the front field. They were all home. We quickly closed the iron gates. And the crowd cheered!

O'mamma declared that everyone had shared a special few minutes of heart- pounding excitement and joy that would not be forgotten, even by the horses.

"It was close to a miracle that they overcame their equine nature," O'mamma said, "and instead of running twenty miles away, they ran back home."

I was proud that the crowd had a chance to see how much they wanted to live with us. The volunteers had run in a few of our footsteps and seen proof of the strong bond of trust and love we have with each other here at Misty Meadows Farm.

We stood facing the fence between us and the church. The crowd was still clapping and waving to us. O'mamma waved back.

With ears perked, I wagged my happiest wag.

Sigh...

ACKNOWLEDGMENTS

J anice E. Keck served the residents of Williamson County, Tennessee as Director of the County Library System from 1979 to 2011. Devoted to increasing our community's connection to the arts, she arranged a wonderful variety of opportunities for writers to further their skills. After many years of working in the field of psychology, I attended workshops at the library and returned to writing poetry and fiction.

Two groups in Franklin, Tennessee provided valuable critique and good company as I developed my storytelling skills. Faith Writers met at Landmark Booksellers and Women Writers at the Coffee House. Members' comments and enthusiasm for Arthur and his stories have had lasting value. I would like to give a special acknowledgement to Sandy Ward Bell for her leadership, spot-on critiques, and enthusiasm for promoting quality in our writing.

Six women, talented in their own fields, deserve the mention of my gratitude for sharing their enjoyment of my poetry and later of Arthur and his wisdom and humor. To Nancy Belser, Bev Bradley, Kathy Budslick,

Penny Case, Caron Haggerty, and Margaret Hall, "What would Arthur say?" He'd say "thank you."

My publisher and friend, Mary Catharine Nelson, has done a wonderful job in producing this book. Her ability to create this presentation of Arthur's stories so well came directly from her dedication to serving the author's purpose. The process would not have been the journey it was without her.

To Bill Corrado, my dear friend, thank you for giving me your vision of the future and for encouraging me to believe in it.

A Ph.D. graduate of Peabody College, Vanderbilt University in Psychology, Louise DeVito was also a long-term student of Pietro Castelnuovo-Tedesco, M.D. and John E. Exner, Jr., Ph.D. Her professional focus has been the evaluation, development, and repair of character to resolve various conditions. Here, she entertains us with the adventures and wisdom of her canine companion Arthur Dogson Todd and the delightful mixture of other personalities on her farm, Misty Meadows.

CPSIA information can be obtained
at www.ICGtesting.com
Printed in the USA
LVHW032257151118
597307LV00001B/1/P

9 781628 802726